Silent Victims

Silent Victims

Hate Crimes Against Native Americans

Barbara Perry

The University of Arizona Press   Tucson

The University of Arizona Press
© 2008 The Arizona Board of Regents

Library of Congress Cataloging-in-Publication Data
Perry, Barbara, 1962–
  Silent victims : hate crimes against Native
Americans / Barbara Perry.
     p. cm.
  Includes bibliographical references and index.
  ISBN 978-0-8165-2596-6 (pbk. : alk. paper)
  1. Indians of North America—Crimes against.
2. Hate crimes—United States.   I. Title.
E98.C87P46   2008
364.15—dc22   2007047751

Publication of this book is made possible in part by the proceeds
of a permanent endowment created with the assistance of a
Challenge Grant from the National Endowment for the
Humanities, a federal agency.

Manufactured in the United States of America on acid-free,
archival-quality paper containing a minimum of 30%
post-consumer waste and processed chlorine free.

13   12   11   10   09   08   6   5   4   3   2   1

To all the people of the world's First Nations

I Walk in the History of My People

—*Chrystos*

There are women locked in my joints
for refusing to speak to the police
My red blood full of those
arrested, in flight, shot
My tendons stretched brittle with anger
do not look like white roots of peace
In my marrow are hungry faces who live on land the whites don't want
In my marrow women who walk 5 miles every day for water
In my marrow the swollen faces of my people who are not allowed
to hunt
to move
to be

In the scars on my knees you can see children torn from their families
bludgeoned into government schools
You can see through the pins in my bones that we are prisoners
of a long war

My knee is so badly wounded that no one will look at it
The pus of the past oozes from every pore
The infection has gone on for at least 300 years
My sacred beliefs have been made pencils, names of cities, gas stations
My knee is wounded so badly that I limp constantly
Anger is my crutch
I hold myself upright with it
My knee is wounded
see
How I Am Still Walking

Used by permission of the author, Chrystos, © 1981

Contents

Acknowledgments

This work has had outstanding support from many quarters, both professional and personal. I must, of course, begin by thanking the many people who shared their stories with me. I can only hope that retelling those stories through this book goes some way toward repaying them for their willingness to spend time with me.

I am especially grateful to Northern Arizona University, my employer during much of the time that I was conducting interviews. In fact, the Four Corners pilot study was made possible by a grant from the university's Intramural Summer Grants Program. The university also supported my sabbatical, during which I conducted the interviews in Montana, Wisconsin, and Minnesota. This latter leg of the project was funded by a United States Department of Agriculture grant (Rural Development Initiative, grant no. 2003-35401-12938).

I am also greatly indebted to many people at NAU. Foremost among these is my good friend and colleague Marianne Nielsen. Her extensive expertise in Native American issues and research was freely given, repaid only in cheesecake. More than that, however, I will forever be grateful for her friendship and encouragement. Linda Robyn was also an incredible support and source of inspiration. I thank her for her insights and advice as I made my way to the Great Lakes region especially. Virtually all of my colleagues in the Department of Criminal Justice supported me in some fashion, but some are due extra thanks: to Larry Gould for his friendship and his advice on Native American issues; to Alex Alvarez for his willingness to share ideas and proofread my work; and to Ray Michalowski for his friendship and for his ongoing willingness to provide advice on all things.

While in the field, I was very fortunate to hire three outstanding research assistants: Paulita Smith (Navajo, Arizona); Matthew Ryan (Ojibwe, Wisconsin); and Ryan Kennedy (Black Foot, Montana). All three did a remarkable job helping me to access participants, understand the communities, and conduct the interviews. Thanks to all of you—I hope the work was as meaningful to you as it was to me. And I hope that it somehow proves to be of some strategic value as you pursue related employment.

Since moving back home to Ontario, I have had the good fortune to once again find myself among incredibly supportive colleagues at the University of Ontario Institute of Technology. Thanks especially to Walter DeKeseredy and Shahid Alvi for helping to keep me motivated and focused.

My editor at the University of Arizona Press, Patti Hartmann, has been an absolute pleasure to work with. She has been there when needed but never interfered or pressured me for a speedy completion. Thanks, Patti, for understanding that sometimes life intervenes! I would also like to include a word of thanks to the anonymous reviewers who made such worthwhile suggestions for the manuscript. It is much stronger because of their recommendations.

On a personal note, there are those in my life who continue to be my strongest supporters and my refuge in times of unbearable stress. I thank all of my family—it is so nice to be so close to home again so that I can enjoy their company. Special thanks to my dad and mum, Keith and Joanne Perry, for their love and support, and for knowing when to spoil me.

It is difficult to find the words to express my appreciation to my husband, Michael Groff. As he would be the first to say, he is my biggest fan. He never fails to encourage and inspire me. This book has been a long time in the making, and he was there for me through it all.

Silent Victims

1
Setting the Context

A student came to my office—a young Navajo woman whom I knew to be struggling financially and culturally to remain at Northern Arizona University in Flagstaff, despite the strong pull to return to the relative security of her family on the reservation. It seemed the past few days had threatened to tip the balance toward going home. For the past three or four afternoons on her way home from campus, she had been taunted and harassed by a group of young white men—presumably also university students—hanging out on their front porch. Their taunts were filled with the standard racialized epithets—"Go home, squaw"; "How many beers today?" The harassment was bad enough, but my young friend also feared that, with time, the harassment would escalate and they would, ultimately, physically attack her. I would come to learn that her fears were not isolated, that many American Indians across the nation shared the same experiences and the same fears. These are, in fact, the forgotten victims of hate crime.

This young woman's story planted the seeds that would ultimately blossom into this book. Following her lead, I began to ask around, to informally pose the question of hate-crime victimization to other students. It quickly became apparent that the problem was perceived to be widespread, in fact a daily reality for many. The Uniform Crime Report (UCR) typically reports in the area of fifty hate crimes perpetrated against Native Americans annually. Without exaggeration, I can say that on any given day, if I were to ask the Native American—mostly Navajo—students in any of my classes about their victimization, the eight to twelve such students in each class could easily catalogue that many among them. Clearly, there was something missing from the UCR's database. As I began to explore further, I realized, too, that it was not just this official source that failed to reflect American Indians' experience. Nowhere in the academic literature could I find references to Native American victims of hate crime. There is, of course, a fairly extensive literature on the collective persecution—in fact, genocide—of American Indian communities; what was lacking was attention to the individualized, daily experiences of racial harassment and violence.

Scholarly attention to the historical and contemporary victimization of American Indians as nations has unfortunately blinded us to the corresponding victimization of American Indians as individual members of those many nations. A review of the literature on Native Americans and criminal justice, and even a similar review of the narrower literature on ethnoviolence, reveals virtually no consideration of Native Americans as victims of racially motivated violence (Nielsen, 1996; 2000a). Bachman's (1992) examination of violence on Native American reservations is silent on the question of intergroup violence. Nielsen and Silverman's (1996) anthology on Native Americans, *Native Americans, Crime, and Justice*, likewise makes no mention of Native Americans as victims of racially motivated crime. The same can be said of Ross and Gould's (2006) more recent collection of essays on Native American criminal justice issues. Barker's (1992) journalistic account of the murders of Native Americans in Farmington, New Mexico, touches on the issue of hate crime but provides no concrete data or analysis.

To be fair, there have been a handful of Civil Rights Commission investigations into discrimination and violence against American Indian communities, but these have been largely regional studies, and the resultant reports have not been grounded in scholarly forms of analysis. Additionally, there has been some limited scholarship on what is sometimes referred to as the "anti-Indian movement," especially by Rudolph Rÿser and the Centre for World Indigenous Studies. (The Midwest spearfishing controversy has been associated with this kind of activity, for example.) However these have been restricted to analyses of quite specific times and places. Consequently, the research on which this book is based was an important endeavor.

In addition to the lack of scholarship, there is also an absence of concrete data on hate crimes against Native Americans. There is no Native American equivalent to the annual audits of anti-Semitic violence or anti-gay violence published by the Anti-Defamation League and the National Gay and Lesbian Task Force. As noted above, federal hate-crime statistics provide little insight. The latest available report indicates that in 2004, there were eighty-three incidents in which Native Americans were victims of hate crime, representing far less than 1 percent of all offenses, and just 2 percent of all those motivated by race (FBI, 2005).

The general limitations of Uniform Crime Report hate-crime data are by now well known and well documented (see Silverman, 1996). Of particular concern at present are two issues: the narrow range of categories of crime, and underreporting. The UCR data reflect only Part I Index Offenses. These represent only eight serious personal (e.g., homicide) and property (e.g., arson) offenses. The report does not include other forms of violence such as harassment; circulating racist, sexist, or homophobic literature; or the use of racial symbols or epithets. Consequently it ignores much of the daily experience of ethnoviolence, which has cumulative negative effects. UCR data, especially the hate-crime data, is notoriously flawed as a result of public underreporting of criminal victimization (McDevitt, Balboni, Bennett, Weiss, Orschowsky, and Walbot, 2000). Fewer than 25 percent of the incidents of ethnoviolence are ever reported, for a variety of reasons ranging from fear of retaliation, to lack of faith in police response (Berrill and Herek, 1992; Cook, 1992). This may be particularly relevant in the case of Native Americans, thereby explaining the low rates of victimization recorded in UCR statistics. In light of the history of Native Americans' conflictive interactions with police, it should come as no surprise that they fail to report victimization to police (Perry, 2006). As the visible and uniformed face of the dominant society, law enforcement agents, even Native American officers, bear the brunt of this suspicion. They command mistrust rather than confidence: "In many respects the relationship between the police and the aboriginal community both reflects and shapes aboriginal concerns about their relationship with government more generally. The police are the first and most frequent contact that aboriginal people have with the justice system and as such often are seen to represent that system" (Canada, Department of Justice, 1991:33). Native peoples are not likely to freely initiate contact with officers who represent a state or a culture that has so often betrayed them.

According to some accounts (Dumont, 1996), the involvement of police in interpersonal affairs is a notion foreign to Native interpretations of justice. To report victimization may be seen as a violation of the traditional value of noninterference with the actions of others (Dumont, 1996). Many, though by no means all, aboriginal peoples share a "reluctance to testify for or against others or him/herself, based on a general avoidance of confrontation" (Dumont, 1996:32). Withdrawal, rather than confrontation, is often the response to hostile experiences. Additionally, the role of police is limited in a culture that values informal community control over formal institutions, and conciliation over retribution (Dumont, 1996).

Finally, the historical and contemporary conditions of powerlessness that are featured later in this book (chapters 3 and 5) have drained many American Indians of the willingness or capacity to confront the dominant white society in response to their victimization. Moreover, the research described here also reveals that ethnoviolence has become a normative part of their lived experience as a people and as individuals. Thus violence seems unremarkable. Additional support for this can be found in Barker's (1992) journalistic account of three Native homicides in Farmington, New Mexico. By way of contextualizing the cases, Barker interviewed people who had been party to "rolling" Indians at the time in question. He concluded that "rolling drunk Indians had been a time honored, if unsavory, tradition among Farmington teenagers for a number of years, almost a rite of passage" (Barker, 1992:173). Barker's interviews revealed that violence against Natives was a typical evening's activity, practiced by a diverse group of young white males. If it was normal for the perpetrators, it may also have come to be seen as normal to the victim community—Native Americans.

Additionally, the available data tends to emphasize the quantitative dimensions of ethnoviolence, that is, the incidence and prevalence. The research described here is significant in that it emphasizes qualitative insights into the dynamics and impact of victimization. Native Americans in this study were questioned about the nature of the violence they have experienced, the context in which it occurred, as well as how it affected them, and how they responded to it, for example. The interviews also explored the extent to which the violence appears to be embedded in broader patterns of discrimination.

Consequently, this book offers a unique contribution to the literature on hate crime. To date, hate-crime literature has tended to be very broad and nonspecific in its focus, and there is not a great deal of scholarship focusing on the specific categories of victims. Extant literature has tended to discuss hate crime in generic terms, as if it was experienced in the same ways by women, by Jews, by gay men, by Latinos/as, by lesbians. Even racial violence is collapsed into one broad category, as if all racial and ethnic groups experienced it in the same way. Consequently we do not have a very clear picture of the specific dynamics and consequences that may be associated with victimization on the basis of different identity positions. The possible exceptions to this are antigay victimization, which has been widely examined by the likes of Gregory Herek (Herek, Cogan, and Gillis, 2002) in the United States; and European work on immigrants (e.g., McLaren, 2003).

Official data and anecdotal evidence both point to the staggeringly high rates of victimization of racial minorities in most Western countries. Despite this, little effort has been made to tease out the effect of racial animus in this context. In fact, it is increasingly the case that racial violence is often inseparable from anti-immigrant violence, given the popular elision between race and immigration status.

The limited data available suggest that African Americans are the most frequent victims of racial violence. Franz Fanon was no stranger to this reality: as an active and outspoken critic of Western racial politics, he often found himself accused of racial transgressions by the white world. Thus he recalls (2000), "I was expected to act like a black man— or at least like a nigger. I shouted a greeting to the world and the world slashed away my joy. I was told to stay within my bounds, to go back where I belonged." It is this normativity that most intrigues me: the extent to which the array of violent practices—verbal taunts, disparate treatment in public and private, assaults, police brutality—continues to be an everyday experience for Native Americans. We might borrow from Georges-Abeyie's (2001) conceptualization of *petit apartheid*, or from Russell's (1998) analyses of micro- and macroaggressions, for example, to further our understanding of the cumulative, ongoing nature and impact of ethnoviolence as experienced by so many distinct communities.

In short, this book is part of a larger literature addressing hate crime as a mechanism of subordination. Additionally, I situate this analysis of anti-Indian violence within the broader and well-developed literature on the historical and contemporary experiences of the oppression of Native Americans. I see hate crime nested within a matrix of social processes that have long produced and reproduced the subordinate status of Native Americans in the United States. Paramount among these, of course, are the processes and practices of colonization that are in fact intended to denude Native Americans of their sovereign status. Hate crime, in this context, becomes a significant strategy by which to remind them of their place should they step beyond appropriate boundaries. The collective victimization that American Indians have so long experienced is by now well documented. However what remains unexplored is to what extent and in what ways their oppression is also manifest in individual experiences of hate crime.

It is this void that I seek to address in this analysis of bias-motivated violence perpetrated against American Indians. I have gathered data from three distinct regions of America, which provides insight into the dynamics of violence perpetrated against American Indians. I began my quest in what was then my own backyard, that is, with a pilot study in the Four Corners region of the Southwest. This would be followed by a survey of Native American students at Northern Arizona University, and a USDA-funded series of interviews in Minnesota, Wisconsin, and Montana.

A number of dominant themes emerged over the course of these interviews—themes that were remarkably consistent across the diverse communities that I visited. Foremost among these was the perception of the normativity of racism and its attendant violence in the lives of Native Americans. There was a widespread sense that they were always vulnerable to the potential for violent reminders of their place in geographical, social, and cultural terms. This seemed to be particularly the case where Native Americans dared to assert their historical rights to land and resources. In such contexts, retaliatory violence became a harsh reality. Furthermore, Native Americans victimized by racial violence often felt that law enforcement offered no protection, in that they failed to take such victimization seriously. In fact, many shared their experiences of harassment and violence at the hands of police officers.

Not surprisingly, the potential and reality of hate crime faced by Native Americans takes its toll on the communities in question. As intended, hate crime plays a key role in the contemporary oppression and segregation of Native Americans. It weighs on its victims, discouraging actions, mobility, and engagement with the broader community. However, increasingly, as Native Americans have become more politicized, it has had the opposite effect, in that ongoing racism and violence actually harden the resolve of communities attempting to reclaim their identities and their rightful place in American society. It is this array of themes that are developed in the chapters that follow.

Outline

The chapter that follows summarizes the theoretical framework and the research project that informs this book. In short, using a model of oppression developed by Iris Marion Young (1990; 1995), I frame Native American experiences of racial violence within a broader array of oppressive practices intended to restrict the actions and power of that community. The empirical base of the book comes from 278 interviews with Native Americans in the Four Corners region, the Great Lakes, and the Northern Plains, in which I queried people on their perceptions and experience of racist violence, as well as the other corresponding forms of oppression.

Before approaching the contemporary experiences of American Indian victimization, I offer in chapter 3 an historical illustration of the links between processes of colonization and racist violence. I argue here that the explicitly genocidal practices of early settlers as well as the more subtle forms of ethnocide in the twentieth century leave a legacy of violence that resonates to this day. Indeed, it is impossible to fully comprehend the current plight of American Indians without paying attention to the colonial history of the relationship between Euroamericans and Native Americans.

Young's model of oppression, noted above, provides a framework for the fourth and fifth chapters, in which I explore the broader experiences of oppression that contextualize and enable hate crimes against Native Americans. Chapter 4 begins by addressing the myriad images that have been used to denigrate Native Americans, thereby justifying varied practices of discrimination and violence. Indeed, the interviews revealed a strong perception among the Native Americans interviewed that the white community, in particular, has had and continues to hold negative and unrealistic stereotypes about American Indians. Similarly, the interviews in chapter 5 uncovered substantial evidence of a wide array of discriminatory and oppressive practices experienced across settings.

Together with archival and census data, the interviews provide insight into the ways in which popular constructs of American Indians as the deviant Other, and structural constraints, provide the context for anti-Indian violence. From the perspective of offenders, the former makes Native people "legitimate" targets; the latter makes them vulnerable targets. Thus chapters 4 and 5, respectively, take up these themes in detail. Together, they set the stage for the violent victimization of American Indians.

Chapter 6 offers an extended discussion of the perceptions and experiences of hate-crime victimization as described by the participants in my research projects. My observations across venues as diverse as Northern Wisconsin and Northern Arizona have revealed some remarkably consistent patterns of racial harassment and violence. One of the most striking themes that emerged was the apparent normativity of racial violence and harassment. Another theme that emerged very clearly in interviews was the extent to which anti-Indian violence was often inspired by American Indian activism. In the name of preserving what few resources have been left to them, Native Americans since the 1960s have engaged in often dramatic politics of resistance. From the occupation of Pine Ridge, to the Northwest fish-ins, to litigation in Euroamerican courts, they have signaled their refusal to be deprived of their last treaty rights. Yet these efforts toward empowerment are commonly met with equally steadfast reactionary mobilizations. Rights claims have triggered reactionary violence from the anti-Indian movement.

Another type of violence revealed in the Native American communities under study appears to come at the hands of state agents, especially law enforcement. The relationship between communities of color and the police has been historically fraught with tension and conflict. The relationship between Native Americans and law enforcement is no exception to this general rule. In fact, police have long played an important role in keeping American Indians in their place.

Having documented the experiences and perceptions of racial violence in chapter 6, I then turn to a consideration of the consequences of this pervasive victimization for individuals and communities. The violence is cumulative in its effects. It is over time that even what appears to be the most trivial of assaults—for example, racial taunts or vandalism— has the most damaging effect. Participants revealed that hate crime in their communities often had its intended effect of oppressing and marginalizing people. In addition, such violence, in turn, has the potential to engender or even increase antiwhite sentiment and activity, as well as internalized racism.

The concluding chapter suggests ways in which Native American communities can be empowered to defend themselves against racist victimization. Importantly, the bulk of these resolutions come from the Native Americans interviewed for this study themselves, and are grounded in their expressed needs and their experiences of what works and what does not work in this context. The suggested interventions range from education of both Indians and non-Indians, to intercultural events, to community mobilization and litigation around rights claims.

2
Thinking about Hate Crime

February 1643, New Amsterdam, New York—Dutch soldiers raid both Wecquaesgeek settlements, ignoring their orders to kill only men, murdering and mutilating Native Americans of both sexes and all ages. Officers report seeing infants dismembered and burned, with others bound to planks before being hacked and stabbed. Corpses are mutilated to such an extent that civilians initially blame hostile Indians for the massacre.

This historical example is a reminder that acts of discriminatory violence and intimidation—hate crimes—are not new phenomena in the United States. It is important to keep in mind that what we currently refer to as hate crime has a long historical lineage (as will be apparent from chapter 3 as well). The contemporary dynamics of hate-motivated violence have their origins in historical conditions. With respect to racial violence, at least, history does repeat itself, as similar patterns of motivation, sentiment, and victimization recur over time. Just as Native Americans of the sixteenth century were subjected to institutional and public forms of discrimination and violence, so, too, are those of the early twentieth-first century. While the politics of difference that underlie these distant periods of animosity may lie latent for short periods of time, they nonetheless seem to remain on the simmer, ready to resurface whenever a new threat is perceived.

Standard statutory definitions of hate crime, like that found in the Hate Crime Statistics Act, share an emphasis on the legal definition of crime. That is, the term *hate crime* assumes the commission of a criminal offense, a violation of an existing criminal code. Such definitions are certainly necessary in the practical world of law enforcement. However from a sociological perspective they are far too restrictive, in that they exclude equally damaging social injuries that may not be considered technically illegal or criminal offenses. The daily occurrences of name-calling, or ostracism of black or Hispanic or Native American youth in the school yard, for example, are not considered crimes from a legal definition; but they are arguably just as damaging in their cumulative impact as an actual physical assault.

This is the standard dilemma in defining crime in general. Crime, hate crime included, is both historically and culturally contingent. What we might define as criminal behavior in one era or one state may not be consistent with those definitions elsewhere. Notions of what constitutes crime are constantly shifting, as we discover new categories of crime and eliminate others. It is thus important, in defining and theorizing any category of harmful behavior, to acknowledge that legal definitions may vary quite dramatically from sociological definitions. Moreover, as the current analysis of racially motivated violence against Native Americans demonstrates, the acts that constitute this particular class of crime run the continuum, from verbal harassment to such extreme acts as assault, arson, and murder. What I am talking about here is not only hate crimes but also what some might refer to as simply hate "incidents." The distinction is important only from a legal perspective. From the perspective of those who experience or anticipate hate incidents as they go about their day, the impact is often indistinguishable. As the literature on domestic violence has shown so strongly, the cumulative effect of being told again and again that one is worthless or subhuman, which is perfectly legal, may be even more disempowering than being physically assaulted on one or two occasions.

Very few scholars have attempted to craft meaningful definitions of hate crime that take into account its social and cultural significance. Wolfe and Copeland (1994:201), for example, contend that hate crime constitutes violence directed toward those who are already disadvantaged by an array of social, political, and economic injustices. This definition is useful in that it acknowledges that the main victims of hate crime are those already marginalized in other ways. Yet it fails to give a sense of how hate crime itself contributes to this marginalization. Sheffield (1995:438), on the other hand, explicitly addresses the importance of the political and social context that conditions hate crime, and highlights the significance of entrenched hierarchies of identity as precursors to hate violence.

Seen in this light, it is evident that hate crime is a systematic effort to keep the Other in line. Hate crime is much more than the act of mean-spirited bigots. It is embedded in the structural and cultural context within which groups interact (Young, 1990; Bowling, 1993; Kelly, Maghan, and

Tennant, 1993; Levin and McDevitt, 1993). It does not occur in a social or cultural vacuum, nor is it over when the perpetrator moves on. Hate crimes must be conceived of as socially situated, dynamic processes, involving context and actors, structure and agency. Hate crime involves acts of violence and intimidation that are not always technically criminal in nature, and that are usually directed toward already stigmatized and marginalized groups. As such, it is a mechanism of power, intended to reaffirm the precarious hierarchies that characterize a given social order. It simultaneously recreates the hegemony of the perpetrator's group and the subordination of the victim's group. Ethnoviolence is directed not only at the individual victim but also toward his or her community. It is a mechanism to intimidate a group of people who "hold in common a single difference from the defined norm—religion, race, gender, sexual identity" (Pharr, cited in Wolfe and Copeland, 1994:203; see also Perry, 2001).

Hate crime can be understood as a means of sustaining boundaries between Us and Them, especially when "they" challenge or threaten carefully crafted sociocultural arrangements; when "they" step out of line, cross sacred boundaries, or forget their place. It is in such a context that hate crime often emerges as a means of responding to the threats. The tensions between dominant and subordinate groups and actors may culminate in violent efforts to reassert the dominance of the former, and the subordination of the latter.

Furthermore, where the popular image of the Other is constructed in negative terms, as is frequently the case for Native Americans, group members may be victimized on the basis of those perceptions. Hate crime is thus "bolstered by belief systems which [attempt to] legitimate such violence" so as to "limit the rights and privileges of individuals/groups and to maintain the superiority of one group" (Sheffield, 1995:438–439). Members of subordinate groups are potential victims *because of* their subordinate status. They are already deemed inferior, deviant, and therefore deserving of whatever hostility and persecution comes their way. In sum, they are caught in a double bind where they are damned if they do and damned if they don't. If they behave on the basis of what is expected of them, they are vulnerable. If they perform in ways that challenge those expectations, they are equally vulnerable.

Hate crime, then, is a forceful illustration of what it is to engage in situated conduct (Perry, 2001). The interactions between subordinate and dominant groups provide contexts in which both compete for the

privilege of defining difference in ways that either perpetuate or recon-
figure hierarchies of social power. This confrontation is informed by
the broader cultural and political arrangements that "allocate rights,
privilege and prestige according to biological or social characteristics"
(Sheffield, 1995:438). Perpetrators attempt to reaffirm their dominant
identity, their access to resources and privilege, while at the same time
limiting the opportunities of the victims to express their own needs.
Committing acts of hate violence, then, confirms the "natural" relations
of superiority/inferiority.

In addition, hate crime might be seen as a form of interpersonal
and intercultural expression that signifies boundaries. The very motive
and intent of racialized violence is to protect carefully crafted boundaries, in the physical and social sense. It is a purposive process of policing
the line between white and nonwhite, between dominant and subordinate. It stands, then, as both punishment for those who dare to trans-
gress, and warning to those who are considering it. This is particularly
significant in Indian Country, where the lines of demarcation have a very
real physical presence. Equally important are the infinitely less predictable, less tangible social borders that "are moving markers, boundaries
that shift according to the positionings we negotiate and build in discursive interaction, in the conversations and actions of social exchange"
(Valaskakis, 2005:250).

The sort of sociological and cultural analysis of hate crime suggested
herein allows us to recognize that it resides in a structural complex of
relations of power. As noted earlier, hate crime does not emerge or oper-
ate in a vacuum. Rather, it is embedded in broader patterns of subjugation and oppression. It is conditioned by structural and cultural practices
that leave its subjects vulnerable to victimization.

Oppression generally, like hate crime specifically, is also more than
the outcome of the conscious acts of bigoted individuals. It, too, is systematic. It represents a network of norms, assumptions, behaviors, and
policies that are structurally connected in such a way as to reproduce the
racialized and gendered hierarchies that characterize the society in question. Young (1990) "operationalizes" oppression in a way that provides
a very useful framework for contextualizing hate crime, and especially
that perpetrated against Native Americans. I use this model as a starting
point for conceptualizing the interrelatedness of the varied forms of subordination experienced by Native American communities since first contact. Admittedly, Young's analysis is directed toward racialized minority

communities, rather than self-conscious nations. Yet it is also the case that the economic, political, and social processes of oppression that she identifies undergird colonization. They provide some of the most powerful structures and processes by which conquering nations attempt to strip colonial subjects of their strength and independence. The historical and contemporary patterns of oppression of Native Americans in particular pose certain problems. Historically, colonial powers—European and American—have struggled to dismantle indigenous strategies of self-government, sustenance, and religious practice, among others, and replace them with Western values. Yet even such "opportunities," as they are considered by Euroamerica, are usually closed to Native Americans. Consequently they are denied both autonomy and inclusion. By subjecting them to foreign political and economic institutions, oppressive practices undermine traditional and preexisting ways of living. For instance, policies intended to geographically or economically marginalize Native Americans, especially where they have been denied the right to engage in traditional lifeways, weakens them individually and collectively.

Young articulates five interrelated "faces of oppression" by which we might characterize the experiences of subordinated communities in the United States: exploitation, marginalization, powerlessness, cultural imperialism, and violence. The first three of these mechanisms reflect the structural and institutional relationships that restrict opportunities for collectives to express their capacities and to participate in the social world around them. It is the processes and imagery associated with cultural imperialism that support these practices ideologically. Together, structural exclusions and cultural imaging leave its subjects vulnerable to systemic violence, and especially hate crime. In short, they provide the contexts in which hate crime can flourish. While I address these contexts fully in chapter 5, I turn now to a brief introductory overview of what is meant by each of these forms of oppression with respect to American Indians.

American Indians and the "Five Faces of Oppression"

Exploitation, from Young's (1990) perspective, refers to processes that transfer "energies" from one group to another in such a way as to produce inequitable distributions of wealth, privilege, and benefits. While typically understood in class terms, the notion of exploitation can also be extended to the conscious efforts of Europeans, and later Americans, to remove Native Americans from their connection to the land and traditional ways of using that land. Like other people of color, American Indians have been forced into wage labor by the advance of capitalism in the United States. Traditional economic practices, whether grounded in trade, agriculture, or hunting economies, have been largely lost. European trading companies, for example, came very early to wrest control of this "industry" from East Coast tribal nations, in particular. Forced relocations to reservations often meant that the other tribes were unable to pursue their traditional agricultural practices on these marginally arable lands. Instead, Native Americans have been left few options but to attempt to play by the rules of a foreign competitive economy. In terms of employment, however, they have typically been relegated to the categories of menial laborers, or even servants. Racialized job segregation persists to this day. When employed, American Indians continue to be overrepresented in menial and low-paying jobs, and dramatically underrepresented in the professions. Consequently, their share of the national income remains low enough to leave a significant number in poverty.

Beyond the exploitation associated with underemployment, there is a lengthy history of resource exploitation (Churchill, 1992; Osborne, 1995), which is a tremendous threat to the autonomy and economic independence of those nations occupying resource-rich land. As a people, American Indians have lost over 95 percent of their land base. Ironically, what is left has been discovered to be laden with valuable natural resources. However, consecutive abrogations of treaty rights to mineral resources, water, and fishing (Robyn and Alcoze, 2006) have all but ceded control of resources to governments and corporations, at the expense of Native economies.

Related to the exploitation of American Indians and their lands is the *marginalization* of Native Americans—the process of pushing them to the political and social edges of society. More so than other American community, American Indians have even been geographically marginalized, first through expulsion into the western frontier, and subsequently by relocation onto reservations or fragmented urban communities (Bigfoot, 2000; Stiffarm and Lane, 1992). Concomitant with this physical separation have been myriad practices intended to expel them from "useful participation" in the economic and political life of society (Nielsen, 1996; Jaimes, 1995). Economically, Native Americans are among the most unemployed and impoverished, and this is even more pronounced on reservations (Taylor and Kalt, 2005).

The marginality of American Indians renders them *powerless* within the context of structural and institutional relationships. Most pressing is the ongoing loss of autonomy of Native Americans (Robbins, 1992; Snyder-Joy, 1996). By virtue of being a colonized people, American Indians were very early stripped of their right to control their own destinies. The attempt to eliminate Native sovereignty was exacerbated by the Major Crimes Act of 1885, for example, which extended federal jurisdiction over felonies to Indian territories. This was followed by over 5,000 additional statutes that extended federal control to Native jurisdictions (Robbins, 1992:93). This political disempowerment, coupled with their economic marginalization, leaves American Indians with little strength with which to exercise the right to freely determine their own political, economic, and social direction.

The federal government's rejection of American Indians' traditions of governance is but one symptom of *cultural imperialism*. Specifically, this dimension of oppression refers to the ways in which "the dominant meanings of society render the particular perspective of one's own group invisible at the same time as they stereotype one's group and mark it as the Other" (Young, 1990:58–59). Since first contact, Europeans, and then Euroamericans, have engaged in this process of "deculturating" Native Americans, simultaneously representing them as inferior beings (Stannard, 1992; Mihesuah, 1996; Jaimes, 1995). It is the long-lasting images of Native Americans as savages, as backward, as uncivilized, or as unintelligent that have facilitated the injustice and oppression experienced by American Indians (Riding In, 1998). With missionary zeal, Euroamericans have persisted in "saving" Native Americans from themselves by repressing traditional folkways, attempting to assimilate them into the dominant culture. Such practices of cultural imperialism have been paramount in the reconstruction of Native Americans as a racialized group, rather than as independent nations.

The structural constraints on Native Americans, together with their construction as the deviant Other, provide the context for anti-Indian violence. The former (see chapter 5) makes them vulnerable targets; the latter makes them legitimate targets (see chapter 4). As noted previously, the collective victimization of American Indians is well documented. Stannard's (1992) work is an encyclopedic survey of the atrocities perpetrated against the indigenous peoples of the Americas. Similarly, the extensive works of Churchill frequently return to the theme of Native American genocide (Churchill, 1992; 1994). In addition, the many accounts of state persecution of American Indian Movement (AIM) members (e.g.,

Leonard Peltier, Russell Means) attest to the use of state power to suppress Native dissidents and activists (see Churchill and Vander Wall, 1990; Messerschmidt, 1983; Crow Dog, 1990). What these accounts fail to address, however, are the mundane, everyday experiences of "random, unprovoked attacks on their person or property, which have no motive but to damage, humiliate or destroy the person" (Young, 1990:61).

It is also apparent that retaliatory forms of hate crime may emerge during periods of activism on the part of subordinate groups. Rights claims of Native Americans have frequently been the motivating force underlying anti-Indian violence. Such incidents of Native mobilization and empowerment are taken as an affront to carefully aligned hierarchies of race and power. Rights claims have frequently been the only provocation for hate crimes intended to reaffirm the powerlessness of Native Americans (Rÿser, 1992).

The Project

The primary aim of the project that informs this book was to conduct the first large-scale empirical exploration of hate crime against American Indians. I conducted 278 interviews or surveys over three phases of research: a 1999 pilot study undertaken in the Four Corners region (funded by the Office of Intramural Summer Grants at Northern Arizona University); a campus hate-crime survey of Native American students at Northern Arizona University; and a 2002–2003 study in the Upper Midwest and the Northern Plains region (funded by the USDA). With the data now in hand, I am in a position to offer a theoretically informed analysis of the experiences of my Native American research participants. I am primarily interested in examining their specific experiences of hate crime; however I also contexualize this violence by taking seriously the ways in which other dimensions of oppression provide an environment in which hate crime can flourish.

Given the exploratory nature of this research, I refrained from stating hypotheses from the outset. Instead, I was guided by a series of research questions that were to a large extent informed by the understanding of oppression and systemic violence—hate crime—offered above:

1. Is Native Americans' victimization isolated, periodic, or ongoing?
2. What is the nature of Native Americans' victimization, and what is its impact?

3. What are the dynamics of ethnoviolence against American Indians? That is, who are the actors? Where does it occur? What is the context of the acts?
4. What is the relationship between ethnoviolence and other forms of oppression (marginalization, exploitation, disempowerment, cultural imperialism)?
5. What are Native Americans' perceptions of the community climate, and the motivations that facilitate hate crime?
6. What role does Native American activism appear to play in motivating anti-Indian activity?
7. What discourages victims from reporting their victimization from police or other authorities?
8. What do Native Americans define as necessary to minimize the impact and the incidences of hate crime?

During visits to American Indian reservations and nearby border towns, I conducted a series of semistructured interviews canvassing Native American experiences of ethnoviolence. There is widespread consensus among scholars who work with Native American communities that face-to-face interviews must be the primary means of soliciting insights from indigenous peoples. For the most part, these communities are grounded in oral tradition. Interviews, therefore, allow information to be gathered in a narrative, storytelling mode that is familiar to participants. Besides, the utility of surveys is limited by the suspicion with which many Native Americans regard the written word. As Marianne Nielsen (2000b) expressed, written surveys "are far too reminiscent of broken treaties." On the basis of her extensive research among indigenous peoples in Canada, the United States, New Zealand, and Australia, Nielsen concludes that

> many Indigenous cultures emphasize oral tradition, and have little regard for written documents. This can manifest itself in a number of ways. The author has been told by older people, for example, that it is disrespectful to take notes during an interview. It may also mean that people will simply refuse to fill out the questionnaire, thereby biasing the non-response rate by excluding people with more traditional values. Because of its highly structured nature, a survey design may also lose the nuances of the data, or miss getting an answer, altogether. (Nielsen, 2000b)

Practically, the use of surveys is restrictive because many Native Americans on reservations, particularly elders, have little or no proficiency in reading or writing English. The interview process, then, ensured the most intensively nuanced responses possible. And in all likelihood, such an approach enhanced participants' willingness to share their stories.

The exception to this practice was a survey I conducted among Native American students at NAU that tapped their experiences of racial violence and discrimination on campus (Perry, 2002). I assumed that, as students, they would be fluent in English, and relatively familiar and comfortable with survey research.

It is also important to note that in each region I hired a Native American research assistant, who helped develop and conduct culturally sensitive interviews. My research assistants ensured that the key concepts would be translated into Native languages. Three interviews were conducted in Navajo by one of my research assistants. The presence of Native American research assistants, typically from the areas in question, undoubtedly helped bridge the cultural distance between the Native American participants and the nonnative researcher. My assistants were also typically students in the social sciences or Native American studies. They might thus be seen as Indian scholars who,

> having grown up in an American Indian culture can provide considerable insight and understanding that may take a non-tribal field worker years to acquire. Furthermore, the knowledge that an Indian scholar might have about his or her own culture often leads to the investigation of issues that non-Indian or non-tribal scholars might not consider. (Champagne, 1998:182–183)

Champagne's characterization proved prescient in this case, as the research assistants definitely facilitated both access to and understanding of the communities we visited.

By its very nature, ethnoviolence is a controversial subject of inquiry. It forces the consideration of individuals' trauma and suffering (physical and psychic), intergroup tensions and conflicts, and chinks in the armor of democracy and egalitarianism. This research faced additional barriers because of the nature of the population involved. Colleagues warned me that I would have great difficulty in gaining access to the Native American community; that Native American people would be unwilling, even afraid, to talk openly about their experiences and perceptions of racial discrimination and violence. There is, of course, a history of exploitation of Native American communities by researchers across disciplines. Too often this has involved "drive-by" research, which according to Nielsen involves engaging in research by taking what can be gotten from the communities but leaving with no thought of returning value or knowledge back to the community in question (see also Bubar and Jumper-Thurman, 2004). Similarly, Champagne (1998:183) argues that the "unhappiness expressed by many Indian communities against scholars, such as anthropologists in the 1960s and 1970s, in part was due to the indifferent way in which data were collected and published, and that resulted in little benefit to the host Indian community." It should come as no surprise then that some Native Americans distrust the motives of researchers. In fact, I came across some cases like this. One woman who ultimately agreed to be interviewed was at first resistant for exactly this reason. It took some convincing to allay her initial suspicion. "Oh, I don't know," she said, "people have been here before; they ask questions, but I don't hear from them again. I don't think they care about us, really."

Fortunately, for the most part we did not meet with extensive reticence on the part of those approached. In all but one of the sites visited, participants were genuinely willing to share their experiences of racial violence and discrimination. In one town, those approached consistently refused to participate; they typically would decline by saying that it would be a waste of time. There appeared to be a widespread sense that whatever was said would have little impact on the lives of individuals or their communities. More common, however, were those instances of people who gladly shared their perceptions and experiences. At one location we literally had people lined up out the door of the office we were using to conduct interviews. Especially exciting were those interviews in which Native Americans expressed strong support for our efforts to uncover what seemed to them to be the invisible and hidden practices of racially motivated violence. These people generally expressed the sentiments of one New Mexico man: "I'm glad you're here. I think this is really important work that no one has wanted to do before. Your questions are welcome here; the answers, I hope the answers will help us here and other Indian tribes, too."

The interviews addressed the dynamics of violent and nonviolent victimization. Thus they reflected the following concepts: hate crime (e.g., verbal insults, harassment, physical violence, dynamics, location); oppression/discrimination (e.g., chronic unemployment); reporting of ethnoviolence; and recommendations for responding to hate crime. I was especially interested in the extent to which violence is perceived to be motivated by recent or current activism on the part of local Native American communities. Additionally, a great deal of time in these interviews was devoted to the question of policies and practices that might enhance relationships between communities, and thus drive down the incidences of hate crime.

The interviews were conducted in seven states: Arizona, New Mexico, Utah, Colorado, Minnesota, Wisconsin, and Montana. Respondents were drawn from eight American Indian tribes representing over a dozen reservations: Apache, Navajo, Hopi, Ute, Ojibwe, Crow, Blackfeet, and Northern Cheyenne. In addition to the 278 Native Americans interviewed, I surveyed a number of nonnative service providers in the regions visited.

Given the wide dispersal, geographically and demographically, of what is known as Indian Country, conducting all of the interviews in the homes of subjects was not a viable option. The travel costs and time required were prohibitive. In addition, there exists no accurate census of Native Americans that could have been consulted to create a random sample. Consequently I employed a combination of convenience and snowball sampling. My research assistants and I spent anywhere from one to two weeks in or near the Native American communities in question, where we solicited volunteers in a number of public locales ranging from Indian centers, to government offices, to public libraries. Others were arranged or suggested by study participants and other contacts in the field. Many of these interviews were, in fact, conducted in the homes of the participants. For the most part then, subjects were in a relatively familiar and unthreatening setting (Grenier, 1998).

As noted above, hate crime is an inherently sensitive research area. The research described herein required very careful ethical considerations. Mihesuah (1996:124) offers a number of guidelines intended to facilitate culturally sensitive research among Native peoples. Consequently, I conducted my research in line with those suggestions that seemed relevant to my work:

Researchers should remain sensitive to the economic, social, physical, psychological, religious, and general welfare of the individuals and cultures being studied. My response to this caveat was to hire Native American research assistants to help with the interviews. This proved very effective, in that it helped to put the subjects more at ease. It also facilitated the solicitation of participants, since the these people were known in the communities we visited.

Recognizing the oral tradition of Native Americans, I relied on face-to-face interviews rather than self-administered surveys. While more costly, it allowed responses from a greater cross-section, albeit a smaller proportion, of the population. It may also have been more meaningful to the subjects who may otherwise have been resistant, even hostile, to the notion of a written survey. The exception here was the mailed survey of campus ethnoviolence that I conducted at NAU. The major assumption driving my use of a survey in this context was that students would be more familiar, and comfortable, with such an approach.

Fair and appropriate return should be given to informants. In line with Native American tradition, I offered reciprocal gifts to all study participants. My research assistants were invaluable in helping me to determine appropriateness in the different contexts, so that such gifts included gift certificates for local grocery stores, tobacco ties, or even a good cup of coffee. Additionally, participants were, in a sense, contributing to change in their communities. By sharing their insights and their hopes for positive action, they shape my work and my recommendations.

The anticipated consequences of research should be communicated to individuals and groups that will be affected. The cover letters and informed-consent material outlined the project and its purpose. Where requested, I elaborated on this statement verbally. And each interview typically ended with a debriefing, during which participants were more fully informed of the possible policy outcomes.

Every attempt should be made to cooperate with the current host society. I have tried to maintain ongoing contact with the appropriate tribal governments and agencies in each community, and with the Indian centers. My intent is to also have copies of this book sent to each of the tribal governments and other relevant agencies in the communities that I visited. I have offered to assist with the development of antihate initiatives and other relevant activities in the communities. I have also helped in the identification of funding sources that individuals and tribes might pursue for relevant projects. At the time of writing, I was actively involved with a number of individuals and organizations in confronting a rash of racially motivated incidents in the Navajo Nation. This included providing resources and filing a report on police failure to effectively respond to anti-Indian victimization.

Geographic Location/Site Selection

There are 286 American Indian reservations in the United States, 511 federally recognized tribes, and approximately 200 unrecognized tribes (Mihesuah, 1996). Obviously it was not possible to conduct interviews in all of these communities. The first leg of the research was conditioned by my living and working in Flagstaff, Arizona, on the edge of the Navajo reservation. Thus the first series of interviews were conducted in the Four Corners region (Arizona, Colorado, New Mexico, and Utah). Beyond that, given that one element of interest in this research was the dynamics of violence in the context of rights assertions or activism in general, this was used as a selection criterion for subsequent visits. In short, research sites were specifically selected for their recent, ongoing history of Native-nonnative conflict. The work of Rÿser (1992, 1993) and of Grossman (1999) in particular suggests that the Indian nations of the Pacific Northwest, the Central and Northern Plains, the Upper Midwest, and the Great Lakes regions have been especially targeted. Consequently I conducted interviews in the Northern Plains (Montana); and the Great Lakes (Minnesota and Wisconsin).

In practical terms, it is hoped that the findings and analysis offered here will yield important policy results. That is, I am interested in informing public policy. The research speaks to quality-of-life issues for Native Americans living in remote rural areas. Many of the conflicts underlying the violence that occurs emerge in the context of land and resource disputes, thus interfering with Native Americans' abilities to pursue their traditional way of life. Understanding these disputes, then, is a first step in resolving them so that Native Americans are free to pursue their interests and their relationship to the land. In the absence of empirical data to characterize anti-Native violence, the Native American communities are not in a position to deal with ethnoviolence. Effective policy depends on data indicating who the perpetrators are, why Native Americans underreport victimization, or where victimization occurs, for example. In particular, the findings may warrant the creation of strategies to encourage reporting; strategies to enhance intergroup relationships, such as diversity curricula in schools; and strategies to enhance police-Native relations, including community outreach and cultural-sensitivity training for police. I am especially interested in what the Native Americans interviewed recommend in the way of antiviolence and antiprejudice initiatives (see chapter 8).

Accurate data on ethnoviolence against Native Americans are vital for scholars, service providers, policy makers, and the Native American community. Consequently, this book will provide some initial data with which scholars and policy makers alike can begin to understand the specificity of the experience of hate crime for American Indians; it will open the door for the emergence of additional literature on this unexplored dimension of racially motivated violence; and it will provide the basis for effective interventions among victims, perpetrators, and the community itself. Information on the nature of such violence, and on reporting practices, will allow for informed organizing and policy making that prevents and responds to the violence that oppresses the Native American population—a theme I take up explicitly in the concluding chapter of the book.

3
A History of Violence
Colonization of America

> Communities have histories of hate, i.e., their own, unique
> organizational institutions, seminal events, and engrained
> attitudes and patterns of behavior.
> (Daniel Welliver, in Flint, 2004:251)

For American Indians, the history to which Welliver refers is grounded
in the legacy of colonialism. In fact, it is impossible to understand the
current strains of Native American racial victimization outside of their
connection with colonialism. Indeed, colonialism is itself an exploitive
and disempowering form of violence intended to disrupt, if not eradicate, its subjects. From first contact, British, French, and Spanish colonizers invested great energy in the debilitation of aboriginal inhabitants
of this continent.

It will be readily apparent from what follows that the historical patterns of colonization experienced by American Indians have followed the
typical modes of conquest, including the suppression and destruction of
Native values and ways of life by the colonizing power, with the intention of forcibly assimilating the colonized group into the dominant society. The process is also associated with the surveillance and regulation
of the colonized by representatives of the colonizers, as by armed forces
or, more recently, by Bureau of Indian Affairs (BIA) or law enforcement
personnel. Moreover, as will be detailed more explicitly in chapter 4,
the associated practices of exploitation and oppression are justified by
a colonizing and racist discourse that insists on the relative inferiority
of the colonized people. In short, colonial practice and discourse were
intended to deprive Native Americans of their status as an independent
people and reduce them to just another racialized group. In fact, one
of the central projects of American colonial history was this very effort
to specifically racialize Native Americans (see, e.g., Saldaña-Portillo,

2001–2002). Yet it is also clear—from the strength of Native American social movements, the persistence of viable treaties, and the continued existence of an albeit depleted land base, for example—that the process was incomplete. As a people, Native Americans have managed to resist the wholesale elimination of their sovereignty.

The practices of colonization have taken slightly different forms over the years since first contact, representing a qualitative shift in emphasis, from genocide to ethnocide. There is an important distinction between the two terms. The former, *genocide*, refers to the explicit and frequently brutal physical violence perpetrated against Native Americans in an effort to eliminate them as a people. There are those who would oppose the use of such strong terminology. Ward Churchill, for example, has come under attack for his persistence in referring to the historical treatment of Native Americans in these terms. However there can be no disputing the facts of history: American Indians have been subject to the full array of practices associated with genocide according to the United Nations Convention on the Prevention and Punishment of the Crime of Genocide (Article 2, 1948). These include

> any of the following acts committed with intent to destroy, in whole or in part, a national, ethnic, racial or religious group, as such:
> - killing members of the group
> - causing serious bodily or mental harm to members of the group
> - deliberately inflicting on the group conditions of life calculated to bring about its physical destruction in whole or in part
> - imposing measures intended to prevent births within the group
> - forcibly transferring children of the group to another group.

It will become readily apparent over the course of the following chapters that each of these measures has been invoked against Native American communities—and some continue to be exercised today. These constitute the most direct and tangible strategies for the elimination of a sovereign people.

The second term, *ethnocide*, refers to the much more subtle efforts to deculturate Native Americans, sometimes through physical violence but more often through the social violence implied in efforts to "resocialize" or "civilize" Natives. In short, colonizing forms of violence run along a continuum and are manifest in multiple conscious acts, such as the introduction and spread of diseases, the forced removal of children to boarding schools, deculturation, and physical punishment for engaging in traditional activities. Each of these constitutes violent means of subjugation.

Whether by violence or assimilationist policy, whites have consistently exerted their energies in the ongoing effort to physically or culturally annihilate Native peoples. Indeed, American Indians were the first to suffer the impact of European religious bigotry in the United States. Initially, the decimation of the Native American population took on the appearance of "unintended consequences" of contact, that is, the massive die-off through the introduction of diseases to which Native Americans had no natural or developed immunity—smallpox, measles, scarlet fever, and venereal diseases, for example. It has been estimated that between 1500 and 1900, Native Americans were subject to nearly one hundred epidemics of European viruses (Stiffarm and Lane, 1992). Increasingly, these epidemics became part of the arsenal of Indian extermination. That infection by disease was official policy is evident in the correspondence of British and American officers of the day. For example, Sir Jeffrey Amherst of the British forces assured a subordinate that "you would do well to [infect] the Indians by means of blankets as well as to try every other method that can be served to extirpate this exorable race." Similarly, a captain in the United States forces wrote in a journal that "we gave them two blankets and a handkerchief out of the smallpox hospital. I hope it will have the desired effect" (cited in Stiffarm and Lane, 1992:32; see also Stannard, 1992; Cook, 1998). Native American vulnerability to disease was exacerbated by concerted efforts to deprive them of their traditional nutrition, such as the destruction of their agricultural lands and the decimation of the buffalo population (Stannard, 1992). Ultimately, hundreds of thousands, if not millions of Native Americans died of starvation, and in fact, whole nations were eliminated.

Willful Violence: The Indian Wars

By the middle of the nineteenth century, Americans appeared to have lost patience with the slow pace of the epidemics in eliminating the Native "threat." Instead, they turned to explicitly genocidal policies and practices, and made no apologies for doing so. Policy makers spoke openly of the need to eliminate once and for all this troubling, savage people. In 1807, Thomas Jefferson insisted that "if ever we are constrained to lift the hatchet against any tribe, we will never lay it down until that tribe is exterminated, or is driven beyond the Mississippi . . . in war, they will kill some of us; we shall destroy all of them" (cited in Stannard, 1992:120). Seven years later, Andrew Jackson would echo these sentiments: "I must distroy [sic] those deluded victims doomed to distruction [sic] by their own restless and savage conduct" (cited in Takaki, 1993:85). And even later, in 1882, a Philadelphia lawyer could still openly raise the same spectre: "We must either butcher them or civilize them, and what we do we must do quickly" (cited in A. Smith, 2005:36).

Throughout the nineteenth century, military assaults on Indian villages became commonplace, especially where the residents had earlier refused to voluntarily give up their lands. Stannard (1992) claims that the intent was patently genocidal, since these villages were often occupied predominantly by women and children during the times when the men were away on hunting or fighting expeditions. As Stannard observes, a population deprived of its women and children cannot long survive. Among the most infamous of these assaults was the massacre at Sand Creek in 1884, where 105 Southern Cheyenne and Arapaho women and children and twenty-eight men were ruthlessly slaughtered by seven hundred heavily armed United States soldiers. In 1890, hundreds of Sioux were slaughtered at Wounded Knee, South Dakota. The tales of white savagery during this onslaught are legion. Those not killed by the powerful Hotchkiss cannons were hunted down and killed in their tracks, even women who bore flags of truce. A Sioux survivor would later recall that "after most all of them had been killed, a cry was made that all those who were not killed or wounded should come forth and they would be safe. Little boys who were not wounded came out of their places of refuge, and as soon as they came in sight a number of soldiers surrounded them and butchered these" (cited in Stannard, 1992:127). In all, these periodic forays accounted for tens of thousands of American Indian lives. Thousands more lives were lost in what policy makers of the day claimed as the more "humane" process of relocation. Those who were removed rather than executed faced an equally grim fate, like the eight thousand Cherokee who perished on the 1,500-mile trek, at gunpoint, from their homeland in the East to Oklahoma. Along this Trail of Tears, nearly half of the original population was lost to exposure, malnutrition, and exhaustion. Similarly, the Navajo's Long Walk, and subsequent internment, claimed 3,500 lives.

The displacement of so many American Indians from their homelands effectively restricted their capacities and opportunities in ways that have left them, quite literally, on the political, economic, and social edges of society. Westward expulsion was accompanied by even more restrictive containment on reservations. These processes of explicit marginalization were noted by some of those interviewed in my study, evidence of the long-term impact of historical processes on contemporary perceptions. It is impossible to understand the current strains of Native American segregation outside of their connection with the isolating effects of colonialism. From first contact, British, French, and Spanish colonizers invested great energy in the marginalization of aboriginal inhabitants of this continent.

The Bureaucratic Assault on Native Americans

Allotment, and its associated practices of assimilation, represented violence by other means. This was a form of bureaucratic assault that was no less threatening than outright physical violence. As Bigfoot (2000:11) frames it, the years between 1880 and 1930 were dominated by "the drive to assimilate Indians into the mainstream of American life by changing their customs, dress, occupations, language, religion and philosophy." Allotment, in particular, would disrupt traditional ways of living in and being with nature, forcing American Indians away from traditional communal forms of land trust, toward privatized and individualized forms of ownership. The epitome of this was the Dawes Act of 1887, which allotted 160 acres to each head of family, or eighty acres to a single person. This resulted in substantial land theft and misappropriation, as dishonest federal agents and land speculators defrauded these newly "landed" Native people of their "property." White purchasers had no interest in the reciprocity of exchange but were interested only in acquiring land with the least possible layout of cash and energy.

Just as the first settlers had claimed that those they had met upon first contact had no idea how to maximize the "use" of the land, so, too, would developers of this era devalue Native abilities to exploit their private property. This would become the beginning of the pattern of "checkerboarding" Indian land, resulting in significant loss of Indian territory. This practice of allotting Native American land to white settlers would later have significant consequences for Native American community unity, and for Indian-white conflict.

Bureaucratic efforts to eradicate the Indian presence once and for all continued apace well into the twentieth century. The federal government made several forays into the realm of terminating all treaties and treaty rights, to alter American Indian status to that of ordinary citizens. By the middle part of the century, more than 200 tribes had been terminated—it was as if they had never existed. The effects are felt to this day in battles for federal recognition. Relocation practices, whereby Natives were moved from their reservations to urban areas, were yet another attempt to assimilate American Indians into the mainstream.

The patterns just described represent an historical trajectory ranging from genocide, to more subtle forms of ethnocide. However the differences among and between the practices were more of degree rather than of kind. The more extreme measures—massacres of villages, infection and death by disease—shared with their less explicitly genocidal counterparts—banning traditional practices, education in Christian boarding schools—the intention of denying Native Americans their culture, their autonomy, and often their very existence.

"For Their Own Good"

The atrocities perpetrated against Native Americans were justified in the noblest of terms (Neu and Therrien, 2003). It was supposedly in the best interests of Natives and colonists alike to separate Native Americans from their lands and folkways. On the one hand, relieving Native Americans of their savage ways would protect settlers. On the other hand, it would also provide Natives with the "civilized" ways that would ensure their survival. Elimination of Native American culture—if not peoples—was the guarantee of progress for all. Nowhere is this clearer, perhaps, than in Andrew Jackson's grand claims:

> The fiends of Tallapoosa will no longer murder our women and children, or disturb the quiet of our borders. Their midnight flambeaux will no more illumine their Council houses or shine upon the victim of their infernal orgies. They have disappeared from the face of the Earth. In their places a new generation will arise who will know their duties better. The weapons of warfare will be exchanged for the utensils of husbandry; and the wilderness which now withers in sterility and seems to mourn the desolation which overspreads it, will blossom as the rose, and become the nursery of the arts . . . How lamentable it is that the path to peace should lead through blood, and over the carcasses of the slain!! But it is in the dispensation of that providence, which inflicts partial evil to produce general good. (cited in Takaki, 1994:64)

As brutal as the history of collective physical violence was the social and cultural violence to which Jackson alludes—all in the name of "civilizing" or "Americanizing" Native Americans. It was, from the perspective of European superiority, a natural right, if not a moral prerogative, to "civilize the savages." And so where genocidal practices left off, ethnocidal practices have waged war by other means. Shrouded in the paternalistic language of assimilation or civilization, an array of practices has led to a significant loss of cultural identity, religion, lifestyle, and governance (Zatz, Chiago Lujan, and Snyder-Joy, 1991). The quantitative devastation wrought by Indian assaults, removal, and relocation is matched by the qualitative devastation wrought by policies of assimilation and deculturation forged primarily through the institutions of church and school. From first contact, white settlers engaged in this process of deculturating Native Americans, simultaneously representing them as inferior, heathen beings (Stannard, 1992; Mihesuah, 1996; Jaimes, 1995). The long-lived images of Native Americans as savages, as backward, as uncivilized, and as godless served as convenient backdrops to the persecution of traditional Native American ways. With missionary zeal, white settlers persisted in saving Native Americans from themselves by repressing traditional folkways and attempting to assimilate them, instead, into the Western, Christian ethos.

Phillip Perlmutter (1999:11) credits Columbus with importing the very tools that would long characterize the colonization of North America's indigenous peoples: "New World war technology, Christian triumphalism, racial intolerance, and massive land robbings." Columbus, in particular, was a typical European religious fanatic, who saw it as his divine duty to eliminate difference through the conversion, conquest, or execution of non-Christians. Subsequent evangelists to the Americas took up Columbus's mission to civilize the Natives by Christianizing them. Even as late as 1899, Senator Albert Beveridge addressed the Senate, proclaiming that "God has not been preparing the English speaking and Teutonic peoples for a thousand years for nothing but vain and idle self-admiration. No! He has made us the master organizers of the world to establish systems where chaos reigns . . . He has made us adepts in government that we may administer government among savages and senile peoples" (cited in Rÿser, 1999 online, p. 9).

It was the image of Natives as savages and wild men that allowed their persecution. Drawing on the emerging notions of social Darwinism, Europeans in the Americas constructed Native Americans as less than human. Some went as far as to characterize them as consorts of the Devil. Rather than acknowledge the validity and richness of Native peoples' spirituality, Europeans characterized them as heathens, to be saved or eradicated. All too often, the latter was the case. In the Spanish Southwest, for example, Pueblo priests risked beatings, even death, if they dared practice their traditional rituals (Mihesuah, 1996).

Clearly the rationale that Native Americans were being civilized "for their own good" provided very light cover indeed for the deeper, less altruistic motives: greed for land and resources. The origins of the modern anti-Indian movement might be seen in the combined doctrines of Manifest Destiny and European superiority, which provided a clear rationale for genocide. Where Native people were constructed as incapable of properly managing their own land, or even their own affairs, it became not just the right, but the duty, of such "advanced" Europeans to claim and then exploit this rich land and all that it had to offer in the way of resources. As we shall see in chapter 7, these land and resource conflicts continue to resonate in periodic episodes of retaliatory violence against Native Americans who assert their rights to their remaining land bases and to nature's resources.

"From Nits Come Lice": Indian Boarding Schools

Nowhere was the Christianizing crusade more evident than in the context of the education of Native American children, which epitomized the long-held assimilationist policy that they must be educated to become civilized. Concomitant with the military conquest of Native peoples was the attempt to disrupt cultural traditions from within through education. For example, in 1617, King James urged American clergy to raise funds for schools for the "education of ye children of the Barbarians"; in 1618, Virginia land was reserved for a "college for the Children of the Infidels"; in 1769, Dartmouth College was founded with the intent of "civilizing and Christianizing children of pagans" (Wright and Tierney, 1991:12–13); and in 1819, the federal Civilizing and Education Act mandated education "for the purpose of introducing among the Indians the habits and arts of civilization."

In 1879, the Carlisle Indian School, the first of its kind, was established by Henry Pratt, whose governing motto was "kill the Indian and save the man." It was in such institutions that Native children would be taught the defining values of white culture, that is, values that would train them perfectly for employment in menial trades: regimentation, reading, writing, arithmetic, the manual trades, and home economics. Over the course of the five to ten years that students attended boarding schools, they would lose—indeed be robbed of—both their mother tongue and their traditional cultural practices.

First through the distant boarding schools, and later through integration into white schools, educators sought to remake Native Americans in the image of the white man. Consequently, students were forced, under threat of severe punishment, to speak only English and practice only Christian religious rituals. They were trained for service in white households and taught to be subservient and deferential when invited into these homes by benevolent white patrons.

It is probably fair to say that historically, schools have not been safe places for American Indians. Rather, they have been coercive, often violent sites for the forced assimilation of Native American youth, wherein their language and culture have been beaten out of them. The history of the "lost generation" of Native American children, shuffled off to BIA boarding schools, is itself a history of violence, intimidation, and repression (Bensen, 2001; Fournier and Crey, 1997). The founder of the Boarding School Healing Project, Sammy Toineeta, refers to the abuses associated with the schools as "one of the grossest human-rights violations because it targeted children and was the tool for perpetrating cultural genocide. To ignore this issue would be to ignore the human rights of indigenous peoples" (cited in A. Smith, 2003:14). Indeed, recall that the forced removal of children from their families and their people constitutes genocide according to the UN Convention cited at the outset of this chapter.

Bigfoot (2000) characterizes the boarding schools as breeding grounds for all forms of abuse, both as punishment and as a means of deculturation. She provides a litany of violations experienced by the children:

- harsh and cruel punishment for behaviors defined as infractions or rule breaking
- whipped and beaten for typical behavior appropriate for children who were scared or frightened
- denied contact with family for months and sometimes years
- denied medical care
- used as indentured servants
- punished for using their Native language

- limitations placed on amount of food, clothing, and shelter they received
- nonnotification of parents upon child's death
- burial on school grounds without markers or ceremony.

In short, the boarding schools were the epitome of colonial education, the goals of which were to deculturate, assimilate, and police the colonized students and, by extension, their communities (Carlson, 1997:137). The heinous nature of the treatment of children was officially acknowledged as early as the 1928 Merriam Report to Congress, and again in a 1930 congressional inquiry into the schools. Nonetheless, neither report had any teeth and consequently did little to alter the boarding-school experience. To this day, the United States stands distinct from Canada and Australia in its failure to officially apologize for the atrocities committed by school personnel. Nonetheless, it can be said that there are those people within the bureaucracy of the federal government who at least recognize the long-term consequences of these violations. Speaking at a ceremony celebrating the 175th anniversary of the Bureau of Indian Affairs, then assistant BIA secretary Kevin Gover had this to say:

> Worst of all, the Bureau of Indian Affairs committed these acts against the children entrusted to its boarding schools, brutalizing them emotionally, psychologically, physically, and spiritually . . . The trauma of shame, fear, and anger has passed from one generation to the next, and manifests itself in the rampant alcoholism, drug abuse, and domestic violence that plague Indian Country. Many of our people live lives of unrelenting tragedy as Indian families suffer the ruin of lives by alcoholism, suicides made of shame and despair, and violent death at the hands of one another. So many of the maladies suffered today in Indian Country result from the failures of this agency. Poverty, ignorance, and disease have been the product of this agency's work.

Sexual Violence as Genocide

Among the forms of violence perpetrated against boarding-school students was the sexual abuse of boys and girls alike. Victimization of women and girls had long been part of the arsenal of violence used to contain Native Americans (A. Smith, 2005), and might in fact be characterized as intrinsic to the processes of genocide and decimation that accompany colonization. An account of the first recorded encounter between European colonizers and an aboriginal woman is telling for its foreshadowing of how Indian women would henceforth be treated as sexual objects:

> I wanted to put my desire into execution but she did not want it and treated me with her fingernails in such a manner that I wished I had never begun. But seeing that (to tell you the end of it all), I took a rope and thrashed her well, for which she raised such unheard of screams that you would not have believed your ears. Finally, we came to an agreement in such manner that I can tell you she seemed to have been brought up in a school of harlots. (cited in Stannard, 1992:84)

A growing body of literature attests to the destructive impact that such violence has on women and on the larger community. A people cannot last long when its women come under attack. The most methodical of the Indian haters, Andrew Jackson, recognized this as a wise military strategy. He encouraged armies to be sure they killed all women and children who could be found after a battle, since it was akin to hunting "a wolf in the hammocks without knowing first where her den and whelps were" (cited in Stannard, 1992:122). In other words, the large-scale murder of women would minimize the reproductive capacities of any given village or tribe. This was precisely what was wanted: to shrink the Indian population to nothing over the course of time.

Stannard (1992) wrote of the widespread rape and murder of Indian women by the earliest settlers, especially among military parties. So, too, does Hurtado (1997) characterize what others have described as voluntary sexual encounters involving Native women as rape, sexual slavery, and prostitution (see also Faery, 1999). Like the land itself, the people—especially the women—were seen as free for the taking. Both nature and its embodiment in Native women were violable and theirs by right (Nagel, 2003; A. Smith, 2005). In fact, the defeat of a colonized people often depends on the conquest of its women, since the latter would remind all that "a woman's proper place was under the authority of her husband and that a man's proper place was under the authority of the priests" (Allen, 1986:87). Sexual assault of the women, then, can be seen as an attempt to minimize the power of men and of the community as a whole. Such efforts helped in the erosion of traditional lifeways grounded in respect for women (and nature), replacing them with European models of patriarchy and the devaluing of women (and nature) (Bubar and Jumper-Thurman, 2004; A. Smith 2003).

As the processes of colonization became even more brutal and more self-consciously genocidal in intent, women would continue to suffer loss of life and dignity at the hands of military troops bent on the destruction of entire communities. This was alluded to earlier in the reference to Andrew Jackson. According to modern literature on human-rights violations against women, this is arguably one of the most heinous ways by which to wage war against the enemy (Bunch, 1995; Nenadic, 1996; Rittner, 2002). Wartime rape of women is indisputably an act of domination. But it is as much about racial and ethnic domination as about gender domination. Rape is not the act of undisciplined individuals; rather, it is a systematic means of humiliating and subjugating a population. It is part of, rather than a consequence of, war, to the extent that rape occurs during military assaults in much the same way that assaults on villages or farms occurs—as a standard means of weakening the community.

Earlier I alluded to the efforts to eliminate Native Americans as developing along a continuum, from genocide to ethnocide, and that the explicit use of violence became less pronounced. However, this same pattern did not apply to the boarding-school experiences of young girls (and young boys for that matter). Here, deculturation, and physical and sexual assaults occurred side by side, with cumulatively damaging long-term consequences for the well-being and integrity of many Native American individuals and communities. I turn now to a consideration of sexual violence as it was experienced in boarding schools.

In her work on gender violence against Native communities, Andrea Smith (2005) pays particular attention to the rampant physical abuse perpetrated against youth, both boys and girls. However she readily admits that much of her analysis is grounded in anecdotal evidence, due to the fact that the violence that permeated the schools as late as the 1980s has remained hidden and undocumented. Nonetheless, she refers to recent cases in the Western states, where priests and educators have faced charges for abusing up to 150 children in each case.

Canadian scholars have been much more effective in uncovering patterns of violence in that country. Given the parallel structures and philosophies of the two systems, there is no reason to doubt that the Canadian findings are also representative of American schools. Fournier and Crey (1997:116–117) assert that "the burden of evidence indicates that more forcible sexual assault has been perpetrated on aboriginal children than on the young people of almost any other nation, except during times of war. The sexual victimization that began as a smoldering ember in the early days of European contact flared to a full blaze during the residential school era."

So traumatic were these experiences for children of an earlier generation that the consequences continue to resonate with the current generation. Many victims of boarding-school violence have committed suicide, or have slowly killed themselves through years of substance abuse as a means of diminishing the pain. Equally tragic are the elevated rates of domestic violence and of child sexual abuse among those who were subjected to sexual violence in their schooldays (Fournier and Crey, 1997)—victims mimicking their victimizers.

In some cases, the damage created by the ongoing sexual assaults on girls was so severe that later they were unable to later conceive. Such inadvertent sterilization, however, was matched, if not exceeded, by the intentional involuntary sterilization of residents, and later, other Native American women. In this we see yet another practice of genocide as defined at the outset of this chapter: the imposition of measures intended to prevent births, thereby reducing the rate of cultural and physical reproduction. Selective practices of eugenics constitute a modern form of gendered violence perpetrated against American Indian women and girls. Consequently, they are stripped of their reproductive rights, and in fact prohibited from reproducing. Even in the modern era, then, overt efforts to manipulate the birth rates of Native Americans have slowed their population growth.

It was not until the 1970s that the extent of this problem came to light. A General Accounting Office investigation in 1976—struck as a result of extensive Native American lobbying—reported that approximately 5 percent of American Indian women had been sterilized between 1973 and 1976 alone. Even more distressing are the estimates of up to 25 percent (Uri, cited in A. Smith, 2005) and 50 percent (Women of All Red Nations, cited in A. Smith, 2005) of all women, depending on the Indian nation, and up to 80 percent on some reservations. Uri, in fact, suggested that all full-blooded women from the Kaw tribe in Oklahoma have been sterilized, thereby effectively killing off the entire Indian nation. In Alberta and British Columbia, whole cohorts of residential-school girls are thought to have been sterilized in the 1920s and 1930s, in accordance with provincial legislation, in a systematic effort to control their sexuality and the population growth of their communities (A. Smith, 2003). Andrea Smith (2005) suggests that this was also likely the case in the United States.

These and subsequent assaults have not, for the most part, been informed and voluntary sterilizations. Rather, they have often been performed in the context of other surgeries (e.g., abortions), or immediately after the women had given birth—certainly not times when they were in a state of mind to freely consent to any procedures. Some women were misinformed about the nature of the procedure (e.g., that it was reversible) or the reason for it. Carpio (2004) describes one woman who was told that her headaches were the result of a fear of pregnancy, and that the only cure was to ensure that it could not happen, that is, to agree to sterilization. Perhaps most disturbing were those cases of very young girls who later recognized that they had been lied to outright. An example:

> I had been sterilized at the age of eleven, at the IHS hospital here in the early 1950s. I got married in the 1960s and I went to the doctor and he told me that I had a partial hysterectomy. When I was a child, they were giving us vaccinations and mine got infected and a nurse came and gave me some kind of shot so I wouldn't hurt. When I woke up my stomach was hurting and I was bleeding. (Woman speaking on radio show *Native American Calling*, 2002, cited in Carpio, 2004:40)

Like Andrew Jackson's soldiers, the physicians and medical staff responsible for the uninformed, often coerced sterilizations have contributed to the decimation of aboriginal communities. With literally surgical precision, they have inflicted parallel forms of violence that minimizes the intergenerational reproduction of communities and culture.

So the modern blends with and imitates the historical. Systemic forms of violence run throughout both the historical and behavioral continua that have characterized the colonization of America. It has been a constant weapon in the arsenal of, first, Europeans, and then Americans, as they have attempted to eliminate the savages from their homelands. And so the violence of conquest set the stage for later patterns of systemic violence that would continue to have far-reaching effects on Native American individuals and communities. In the chapters that follow, I explicitly take up the persistent patterns of stereotyping and structural constraints that contextualize contemporary forms of hate crime perpetrated against American Indians.

4
Imaging American Indians

Embedded in and transcending the history I have just described are myriad patterns of cultural imperialism that both trivialize traditional indigenous knowledge and construct Native peoples as inherently inferior. To experience cultural imperialism, according to Young (1990:81), "means to experience how the dominant meanings of a society render the particular perspective of one's own group invisible at the same time as they stereotype one's group and mark it as the Other." Typically, anti-Indian sentiment and activity is framed by cultural imaging of the subordinate group. Within such constructs, the values and experiences of the dominant group typify the norm, while subaltern groups are rendered invisible at best, deviant at worst. These trends also lend permission to hate, in that they imply the Native Americans are not fully worthy of respect.

The racialized images that will be discussed in this chapter have been invaluable to the processes of colonization. They are, in fact, inseparable, to the extent that the dehumanizing caricatures of Native Americans provided powerful rationales for colonial practices that denied the sovereignty of a people, as well as their related claims to their homelands. Racism—colonial racism to be more specific—is both a support for and an outcome of a legacy of colonization that has sought to eliminate the political, cultural, economic, and territorial autonomy of Native Americans.

Colonial rule operated in part by constructing both discursive and institutional systems of difference and hierarchy. It thus required the "naturalization" of hierarchies, in this case, grounded in race, by which the colonized and colonizer could be distinguished. The related ordering process reinforced proscribed relations of inferiority and superiority. Colonial discourse thus racialized an autonomous people. Wherever possible, colonial authorities would respond to Native Americans, not as sovereign people, but as inferior racial beings.

Colonial racism specifically exploited the emerging "science" of race, that is, social Darwinism, to reduce a diverse people to their racial features, relying heavily on racial imagery and emerging stereotypes to do so. This discourse of race, created and reproduced by white Europeans, defined Native Americans as incapable of self-government; as childlike, uncivilized, or backward by turns. In so doing, the socially constructed hierarchies of race could be used to lend legitimacy to otherwise heinous practices of ethnocide and genocide. Social Darwinism would also provide the needed justification for exploiting the newly discovered land and its resources. Where the racialization of African Americans provided justification for their use as chattel, the racialization of Native Americans would allow unencumbered exploitation of their land and resources, as well as the denial of their nationhood.

Since first contact, Europeans, and then Euroamericans, have engaged in this process of representing Native Americans as inferior beings (Stannard, 1992; Mihesuah, 1996; Jaimes, 1995). It is the long-lasting images of Native Americans as savages, as backward, as uncivilized, or as unintelligent that have facilitated the injustice and oppression experienced by American Indians (Riding In, 1998). Euroamericans have taken it upon themselves to rescue Native Americans from their backward ways, by repressing their rituals, beliefs, and means of survival, forcing them instead to adopt white ways. That these images continue to inform nonnative perceptions of American Indians was evident throughout the interviews. Many of those interviewed were very much aware of the stereotypes that framed their interactions with others.

> I think a lot of it is based a lot in ignorance. That sounds connotative—lack of information, stereotypic ideas. Maybe their form of it might come from their parents and grandparents. Indians are drunks, they're lazy, they're wasteful. I think this is something that is in the minds of some people, not everyone. (Utah, female)

The legacy of cultural imperialism runs deep, continuing to inform Native-nonnative interactions. Much of white America clings to the remnants of the mythologies of Manifest Destiny and white supremacy—albeit in somewhat muted forms—to justify its (mis)treatment of American Indians. According to their mantra, the land and its resources are theirs by right, and anyway, Native Americans are incapable of using the land efficiently; Native Americans are savages, they're lazy, they're dependent, they're unfairly privileged, they're in need of white protection and guidance. It is in the name of these sometimes hostile, sometimes paternalistic sentiments that Native Americans have been, by turns, massacred, deculturated, exploited, and assaulted. The associated imagery creates an outcast minority, thereby legitimating the varied forms of oppression and degradation imposed on them.

This is a typical strategy for marginalizing, if not stigmatizing, the Other. The realm of stereotypes and popular images justifies and underlies the hostile treatment of racial minorities. In line with an essentialist understanding of racial classification, the overriding ideology is that of inscribed traits, wherein "the stereotypes confine them to a nature which is often attached in some way to their bodies, and which thus cannot easily be denied" (Young, 1990:59). The very process of racializing Native American communities is itself essential to the denial of nationhood. Hundreds of self-sufficient, autonomous nations are reduced to a single homogeneous collective, called "Indians." They are reduced in status to just another minority group, sharing undifferentiated characteristics, and typically unflattering characteristics at that.

Stereotypes that distinguish the racialized Other from white people are grounded in what are held to be the identifying features of racial minorities. They thus help whites to distance from nonwhites. The latter are to be feared, ridiculed, loathed for their differences as recognized in the popular psyche. Almost invariably, the stereotypes are loaded with disparaging associations, suggesting inferiority, irresponsibility, immorality, and nonhumanness. Consequently, they provide both motive and rationale for injurious verbal and physical assaults on minority groups. Acting on these interpretations allows dominant group members to recreate whiteness as superiority, while castigating the Other for their presumed traits and behaviors. The active construction of whiteness, then, exploits stereotypes to legitimate violence.

Once identified as such, no minority racial group can escape the application of labels that are applied to the group as a whole. Most communities of color share the unfortunate fate of being characterized as dishonest and deceitful. In some cases, this takes on the extreme of painting the whole group, especially males, as criminal; as violent, thieving, sexual predators. Several racial groups, Native Americans included, are also identified as lazy and unambitious. The high unemployment rates of these groups are taken as a sign of their unwillingness to work, rather than the structural discrimination that precludes them from rewarding, high-paying jobs. There is an historical continuity that underlies these images; they are not simply new labels pinned to an ancient people. Rather, they derive from historical patterns of representation.

An Historical Legacy

Modern stereotypes are in fact defined by long-standing constructions of who and what American Indians are perceived to represent. However these constructions are characterized by a certain level of ambiguity. Is the accent on *noble* or on *savage*? Are they to be seen as innocents in nature, or violent by nature? As Valaskakis (2005:127) puts it, "Indians have always been vagrants in the historical, political, and popular impressions of the Western frontier. The discourse of the Indian as noble and savage, the villain and the victim . . . is threaded through the narratives of the dominant culture and shifting perceptions of the western frontier as a land of savagery, or land of promise." In one breath, for example, Columbus referred to this "new people" as "very gentle and without knowledge of evil" (cited in Takaki, 1993:32). Yet how can we reconcile this with his mistreatment of those who so welcomed him? While finding them guileless, he nonetheless set his troops loose on the unarmed Natives on more than one occasion, slaughtering men, women, and children by the hundreds (Stannard, 1992).

At first contact, fear of the unrecognizable Other quickly changed to grudging respect, as coastal Indians offered guidance and assistance to the newcomers. Here, thought the English settlers, were a truly generous and gentle people—so thought the European colonists as long as Native people were helping them, to find precious resources, or clear the land, or defend them from other, more hostile tribes or nations. However, as the greed for land and territory increased, so, too, did hostility for its original occupants, who now came to be seen as superstitious, savage, and uncivilized (Vaughan, 1995; Perlmutter, 1999).

It would be these less flattering accounts of what John Smith referred to as "cruel beasts" that would henceforth dominate the characterizations of North (and South) America's First Peoples. Even where pity for their loss of land and clanspeople might be evoked, American Indians were nonetheless blamed for their own plight. Their defensive tactics were taken as evidence of their base savagery and violent natures. Europeans, after all, were merely trying to help Native people develop and prosper according to European standards of what that implied.

Such paternalistic rationales for the genocide of American Indians rested on the genuine conviction that Europeans were in all ways superior to this newly "discovered" race. In the first instance, it is readily apparent that European colonizers have continued to disregard or minimize the value of indigenous knowledge, that is, the traditional, local knowledge of how best to live in and with nature in the immediate environment (Grenier, 1998:2). These types of knowledge systems represent generations of cumulative wisdom based on direct observations and experiences. The very survival of Native peoples on all levels has depended on their being able to utilize knowledge in balance with the natural environment.

Historically, those seeking to exploit valuable resources failed to draw from this vast wealth of indigenous knowledge. The legacy of fifteenth-century European colonial domination relegated indigenous knowledge to the categories of primitive, simple nonknowledge, or folklore. This is, no doubt, closely tied to the related principles of *territorium res nullius* and *vacuum domicilium*. Both tenets implied the capitalist notion of uninhabited land, that is, "unused" land. From the perspective of colonists who had, in part, fled Europe due to overpopulation and overdevelopment of the land, the North American continent must have appeared underused at best. John Winthrope, for example, claimed that New England Natives "inclose noe land, neither have any settled habytation, nor any tame cattle to improve the land by," and so could make no legal claim to the land. Even the Supreme Court would weigh in on the matter, arguing that "the tribes of Indians inhabiting this country were fierce savages, whose occupation was war, and whose subsistence was drawn chiefly from the forest. To leave them in possession of their country, was to leave the country a wilderness" (United States Supreme Court). This is also a philosophy of which modern Native Americans are aware, as the following suggests:

> That Indians are part of the wild part of the West, have to be tamed, have to be pushed, because they'll never be fully humans, cause they're part of nature. 'Cause they think that it belongs to all of them. Yeah, it's the mentality, I mean, it's been maintained, it's Western mentality that's been continued, and the West is violent, always has been. (Montana, male)

However, to regard the land as unused is to deny the sophisticated and sensitive approaches to land, resources, and nature as generally practiced by Native inhabitants. Valaskakis (2005:97) sees these tenets as social constructs that help "empty the land, justify its occupation, and underwrite policies to exterminate or acculturate Indians." It comes as no surprise, then, that through the processes of colonization, indigenous knowledge and perspectives have been ignored and denigrated by colonial powers seeking to exploit indigenous resources.

Consider the example of the Chippewa of the Great Lakes region. The fishing-rights struggles in Wisconsin, which began in the 1980s, are rooted in the origins of the Ojibwe (or Chippewa) people and their relationship to the environment of the Great Lakes. Clan laws among the Chippewa and other woodland peoples must be obeyed by all to achieve peace and harmony in the community (Fixico, 1998). Most woodland peoples like the Chippewa, who have clanship systems and clan laws, believe these laws must be obeyed to avoid disrupting natural relationships with the environment. Failure to adhere to these laws will bring both human and natural calamities (Fixico, 1998). From this perspective, the overfishing of which they were accused by the anti-Indian movement was an unlikely problem: the Chippewa were well aware of just how destructive overfishing would be to the entire culture. Despite claims made by the anti-Indian movement in Wisconsin, treaties do not allow the Chippewa to deplete the resources, as anti-Indian groups would have people believe, but rather to protect the land and all the creatures in and on it, according to traditional knowledge and practice. Antitreaty activists frequently made the claim that Indian spearfishing threatened the Great Lakes fish populations, when in fact their approach ensured healthy water, lakes, and wildlife.

This failure to recognize the value of indigenous knowledge was noted by one participant, who observed,

> We need to educate. I think we need to shift a gear, make response, get attuned to the fact that we haven't done enough. The stories need to be told—our stories, our histories, from our perspective. . . . We need to acknowledge, we need to remind that Indians came first, that they have a history, stories. Then you would understand that if it wasn't for them, you wouldn't be here, 'cause they helped you. (Wisconsin, male)

Yet another common image associated with Native Americans has been the perception that traditional life for Native peoples worldwide is simple or primitive. However, when we examine the cultures or societies of Native peoples in the Americas and other areas around the world, we uncover high levels of sophistication and complexity that have been integral to their success as nations. The assumption that the people of the Americas were primitive, uncivilized savages is simply untrue. If we put aside our fascination with technology and material wealth, we find that for many people in modern Western society, life is primitive and stunted in terms of family values, spiritual life, commitment to the community, and opportunities for rewarding work and creative self-expression. These are the very areas most richly developed in traditional communities of the Americas.

The contrasting value systems of Native America and the Euroamerican capitalistic values of power, materialism, economic efficiency, and immediacy have led to confusion and misunderstanding about other people and their ways. Euroamerican views toward family and religion are different from the views of many American Indians. While not all Euroamericans are of the Christian religion, much of the knowledge contained in the exploitive dynamics of the Christian religion is closely tied to the philosophical concepts underlying our capitalistic society. Christian capitalism, therefore, is not connected to the earth or environment like the spirituality of "the Way" of American Indians (Tinker, 1993). In this context, the unequal balance and hierarchical social structure produced by the expansionary needs of capitalism is, to many American Indian people, highly destructive to their perception of the need for balance between physical and spiritual worlds.

When asked what they thought were the underpinnings of anti-Indian resentment, a number of study participants suggested that one contributing factor was this very tension between the imposition of Western values on Native American cultures—in short, cultural imperialism. This sentiment is made clear by the following observation:

> Everything falls on the Native community to bridge gaps and make the community better. This is really another form of that dominance-subordination power relationship that goes on. Besides, most whites don't care to know. It is a position of power to be ignorant. One group has to know everything about their society and the other group's society just to survive it, but the other group doesn't have to know anything about the first group. A classic colonial relationship. The latter group determines all the rules and all the means and the former must struggle to fit in. (Arizona, female)

On one level, one could take issue with this woman's interpretation. Contemporary white Americans supposedly know a great deal about Native Americans. The problem is that what they know is inaccurate at best.

Imaging Indians Today

Devon Mihesuah's (1996) *American Indians: Stereotypes and Realities* provides a catalogue of dominant stereotypes that continue to frame popular perceptions of Native Americans. She opens her analysis with the assertion that

> no other ethnic group in the United States has endured greater or more varied distortions of its cultural identity than American Indians. Distorted images of Indian culture are found in every possible medium—from scholarly publications and textbooks, movies, TV shows, literature, cartoons, commercials, comic books, and fanciful paintings, to the gamut of commercial logos, insignia, and imagery that pervades tourist locales throughout the Southwest and elsewhere. (Mihesuah, 1996:9)

A woman from Minnesota echoes Mihesuah's observations on the diversity and pervasiveness of popular misconceptions, based on her own experiences:

> That's been, that sort of self-righteousness, so in the old days it was, well, all the Indians were on welfare, they all get this welfare, they all get that government check. And we pay for that. There are millions of people who have made millions of dollars off of Indian resources in this country. But it doesn't sink in, you know? And the problem with most people's sense of history, both about this country and about Indians, is it's like a TV commercial. So they, so we're dealing with an ignorance that's just hard to overcome. You know? It's so systematic, and it's so much a part of people's minds about Indians, and it's that self-righteousness.

Mihesuah gives substance to the assertions about the social constructs associated with Native Americans, identifying and refuting twenty-four dominant stereotypes—stereotypes that inform and justify denigration and harassment of Native Americans. Four clusters of American Indian imagery seem especially noteworthy. As we saw in the previous section, since first contact, American Indians were thought to be without a recognizable culture. They were deemed to be uncivilized savages who showed no signs of social, political, cultural, or religious sophistication. Rather, they were from the outset perceived to be disorganized, warlike, and wasteful of the land and resources available to them.

Of course, nothing could be further from the truth. The precontact tribes as well as those that have survived to this day were and are rich in all aspects of community life. They are more accurately characterized as having "sophisticated systems of government, community organizations, economy, means of communication, gender roles, arts and elaborate clothing and hairstyles. Indians were and are extremely religious; ceremonies and rituals were and are a part of their daily life" (Mihesuah, 1996:431). If there is any truth to the myth of an uncultured people, it is more a reflection of the processes of deculturation associated with colonialism than it is of the inherent capacities of Native American communities. For one woman interviewed, this stereotype boils down to an inability, indeed an unwillingness, to truly try to know and understand Native American cultures:

> That's the kind of thinking that's been going on from the very first contact that we ever had with non-Indians, and that perception has never changed. It's just always been the fact that, you know, we're different and we're not like them, we're never gonna be like them, and I don't think you like us, and that kind of stuff, and so that thinking is sort of all thinking and dialogue between Indians and non-Indians. (Minnesota, female)

It is perhaps no surprise, in light of this observation, that Native Americans are also perceived to be incapable of progress. This is most clearly evident in what Mihesuah identifies as the related myths that Native Americans have made no contribution to America, and that they are a "vanished race." Native Americans I interviewed were very much attuned to the idea that their culture was perceived to be regressive and constraining, rather than enabling:

> When I was in Dakota, what I used to hear was "your culture is not going to help you succeed in the Anglo world, so why do you bother," and you were taught [that] to succeed, to be a productive member of society, you had to act Anglo . . . And at the boarding schools, and Chinle had basically the same attitudes. "Where is your, your tradition, your culture going to get you in this Anglo society?" (New Mexico, males)

Even high-school students recognize that they are perceived as less capable than their white peers, as one young man from Minnesota noted: "'Cause the teachers, teachers, like, I don't know, they'll give you a test and they think you already, like Indian already failed, it's a waste of time, like we're stupid or something. They don't think we belong in a white world or something." To conceive of Native Americans as incapable of making contributions on their own merits is to deny the past and present ways in which American Indians have shared both traditional and contemporary expertise with Europeans. Curiously, this was something President Richard Nixon even admitted in 1971, as he addressed a Congress on Indian Affairs:

> The story of the American Indian in America is something more than the record of the white man's frequent aggression, broken agreements, intermittent remorse and prolonged failure. It is a record also of endurance, of survival, of adaptation and creativity in the face of overwhelming obstacles. It is a record of enormous contributions to this country: to its art and culture, to its strength and spirit, to its sense of history and its sense of purpose. (cited in Reyhner, 1993:63)

Historically, American Indians have also offered much in the way of agriculture, medicine, environmental conservation, resource development, military service, and democratic processes. Despite efforts to disempower Native Americans, they continue to play key roles in the arts, politics, criminal justice, and academic scholarship, to name but a few fields. These are not the activities of a backward or defunct people. On the contrary, as the concluding chapter will demonstrate, Native American communities are undergoing a rapid and wide-ranging reemergence as a driving force in America.

Despite the reality of Native American productivity, there remains a widespread belief that they are not self-sufficient but are instead dependant on the state for their survival. Everyone supposedly knows they get free handouts of cash, scholarships, vehicles, and food. Everyone knows they don't work but rely on welfare to support their many vices:

> Yeah, it's really appalling, some of these white people have lived here for generations, and they're still like, "They don't pay any taxes." They're still saying, "They get free trucks, their government gives them free trucks." What? It's like a part of a mythology, or a fantasy, like we're better off, and it's an excuse to rip us off for loan interests and stuff like that. And, well another thing, the idea is thought among some, "Oh, the more money they have, they'll just spend it on

liquor." To some extent you hear, "They just spend it on junk food, look at the diabetes rate." (New Mexico, male)

No other ethnic group has been so consistently maligned for leeching on the largesse of a benevolent state. The irony, of course, is that such assertions "sound ridiculous to many Indians who live in terrifying poverty with no transportation, no running water, electricity or phones (though some don't want these things), and who receive little, if any, assistance from the government" (Mihesuah, 1996:87). Native Americans are no more or less inclined than similarly situated (that is to say, impoverished) white people, black people, or Asian people to receive government assistance. Payments they might receive directly from the federal government are typically connected in some way to treaty requirements—lease revenue, or gaming revenue, for example. These are funds owed to eligible Native Americans in exchange for land ceded during prior treaty agreements. They don't reflect "special" rights but rather legally binding treaty rights.

Underlying the varied myths of Native American backwardness is a final cluster of stereotypes that generally paint Native Americans as morally and intellectually inferior. Elevated school dropout rates, substance abuse, and unemployment are seen as causes rather than effects of their marginalized status. An apt illustration:

"Well, they can't handle that job, they're lousy drivers, they can't handle the job, they're lazy, they're drunks, they . . ." Oh, I remember a Christian in the Assembly of God church, that said, because they sleep in a hogan, and the children get to watch their behavior, that they shouldn't be allowed to come to the Sunday school and be part of that group. (Arizona, female)

As in this case, Native Americans believe they are blamed and ostracized for their own social problems, which are deemed to be rooted in their very natures. This occludes the structural mechanisms that leave far too many urban and rural American Indians on the fringes of society (see chapter 5). Consequently, media, politicians, and popular discourse perpetuate the myths that portray Native Americans as morally bankrupt, lazy, deceitful, and alcoholic. As is typical of stereotypes generally, this image in particular is relatively immutable, even in the face of counterevidence, something noted by one woman from Minnesota:

It's the way stereotypes are. People that have 'em, I mean, you could line you and I up and all of our students in a line, and sober and motivated and educated and all that, and you could have lined up in a row successful men. And you could have one Indian walk by who is staggering, with long hair, and they say, "Now that's an Indian." And that's the perception, you know? It just hangs on and hangs on, because stereotypes are like that.

This is by no means an exhaustive rendering of the many pictures that inform the public imaging of Native Americans. It is, nonetheless, an overview of the dominant themes that establish Native Americans as somehow less worthy of respect. As such, these and other largely pejorative stereotypes "promote injustice, disrespect, oppression, unequal treatment, and genocide. They keep people from understanding differences, similarities, problems, and potential solutions" (Riding In, 2002:25). In short, contemporary images of Native Americans continue to provide a rationale for both historical and modern practices that stigmatize and exclude them. This may help to explain, also, the absence of Native American issues in school curricula: for just as they are deemed not worthy of respect, so, too, does it appear that they are not worthy of mention in educational settings.

Not in the Books

We were having a discussion in class on why Natives are excluded from American history, you know, when you spend so much time lionizing your heroes and telling the same old predictable story about how they went out against overwhelming odds, and of all these obstacles, and then in the end they're shining heroes . . . The last thing they want to do is talk about contributions of Native Americans and our bloody legacy and the millions that were decimated and killed, and famine, disease, and government policy termination, you know, that's not the type of thing you want to teach your American kids. The educational system that force-feeds us this bullshit. A lot of these, a lot of these, and I feel kind of bad for white America because it, you know, it doesn't promote any kind of culture. (Minnesota, male)

Earlier in this chapter, an interviewee was quoted as saying that "most whites don't care to know" about Native American culture, knowledge, or history. This is most telling in the invisibility of Native American issues in education and in educational materials. While it is true that traditional indigenous knowledge is typically overlooked or rejected outright, parallel to this is the tendency to offer limited—and often inaccurate—information about indigenous peoples. Two young women, still attending high school, made some startling comments about this:

> How about in your history classes? Do you get much about Native American contributions to history?
> Not really. They talk about the war, immigration, all that.
> Not much culture. I don't like the fact that, you know, we're pushed into their culture, and they can care less about ours. (Minnesota, females)

The last comment, in particular, highlights the extent to which cultural imperialism infects the delivery of curricula in public schools. Too often such curricula continue to render Native American peoples and their contributions to American society invisible. Education resembles a one-way street, wherein Native youth learn about the dominant culture, yet neither they nor their classmates learn much about Native American culture (Reyhner, 1993). If one were to judge the place of American Indians within American culture, one might think that they have existed only in the East, and only during the first few decades of European settlement. Beyond these spatial and temporal boundaries, Native Americans are rarely seen in educational materials. Indeed, "students still learn in first grade that Columbus 'discovered' America, a land sparsely populated by heathens who had nothing to contribute to the world except corn" (Mihesuah, 1996:11).

Troubling as it is that American Indians are so little acknowledged in the public schools, there is added reason for concern when even those schools with sizable concentrations of Native students similarly pay short shrift to American Indian issues. Many Native Americans in my interviews had very strong perceptions that their own children were getting very little in the way of education on traditional culture, beliefs, even language in schools. This was especially the case in border towns like Blanding, Utah, and Bemidji, Minnesota, where respondents had this to say:

> What kind of subjects, what's missing there?
> I would say, just like I mentioned, elementary, junior high, if they come out with a junior high, they should just focus on junior-high classes and then high school over here, and I think they should have more, like, Navajo language courses, or history. They don't teach

much about our culture. Our kids don't know, white kids don't know. (Utah, female)

There's Ojibwe classes, and you can take classes on all that.
    How about in, in other classes that aren't specifically Ojibwe classes or something, like in your other social studies, do you learn a lot?
    History, I suppose, I would guess.
    You would guess?
    Yeah, you know, it's more on the Romans and Greeks, I mean. Ancient civilizations elsewhere, not here, not us. (Minnesota, male)

This is not to say that attention to American Indian culture, history, and language is entirely absent. On the contrary, there is reason for hope, in that reservation schools, in particular, are taking pains to integrate more accurate and positive Native American curricula. When asked, many Native people responded that they or their children were being more self-consciously immersed in American Indian cultural lessons. This has been facilitated by such federal initiatives as the Native American Languages Act (1990) and the Indian Nations at Risk Task Force (1991). The latter reported the belief that "a well-educated American Indian and Alaskan Native citizenry and a renewal of the language and culture base of the American Native community will strengthen self-determination and economic well-being and will allow the Native community to contribute to building a stronger nation" (Indian Nations at Risk Task Force, 1991:iv). To this end, one of the goals called for by the task force was to provide Native students with the "opportunity to maintain and develop their tribal languages" as well as to "create a multicultural environment that enhances the many cultures represented in the school" (Indian Nations at Risk Task Force, 1991). As will be discussed further in the concluding chapter, the introduction of American Indian lessons in schools is a necessary and progressive step.
    Nonetheless, the integration of such education has been hit and miss. Plus it is not without its detractors. Even where Native American issues are pressed onto the educational agendas of nonnative schools, there is the potential for resultant resistance by whites. This is reminiscent of the statement by the young student above: "We're pushed into their culture, you know, and they can care less about ours." Teachers, parents, and students have blatantly demonstrated their disapproval of forced education on Native American issues: "Natives continue to use education to decolonize, and their efforts continue to be thwarted. In present-day

Montana, some white parents at the Flathead Reservation removed their children from a class on Native Americans, charging that an 'un-American' curriculum was offered" (Ross, 1998:67). A similar rebuff met Indian students in Hardin, Montana, where they had planned a one-day conference, what has been described as a powwow intended to celebrate their culture. One Native American man described the response of the Anglo population of this border town in the following exchange:

> In Hardin, this may have been six or seven years ago now, has to be seven years ago now, on Native American Day, the Native American Club wanted to have an all-day powwow singing or whatever, and the majority of whites either didn't show up, or if they did show up, they left school early, and so then the truant officer tried to enforce truancy, and so the parents said, "Why are you trying to force our kids?" and it just got uglier, and one of the Indian parents that I know, who is pretty vocal, went to the school, and the principal spit on him, he said, "What are you doing allowing this type of racism to . . . ?" He's not from here, he's from North Dakota, which is much better, but, yeah, and it's so ingrained.

Such willful rejection of the opportunity to learn about and from American Indian communities only reinforces the ignorance of nonnatives living in communities like this. In the absence of dedicated attention to the realities of who Native Americans are, what they have accomplished, and how they practice their culture, too many people fall back on outmoded and offensive stereotypes to construct their mental images of these diverse communities. This becomes an especially important issue in the concluding chapter, where I discuss the ways in which educational reform might act as an inoculant against the imagery that conditions racially motivated hate crime against Native Americans. Confronting and challenging—at an early stage—such narrow and disparaging stereotypes as have been discussed in this chapter provides one avenue by which the distance between Native and nonnative communities might be reduced. In the meantime, popular misconceptions of Native Americans continue to inflame hostility toward them.

Implications for Hate Crime

In her recent book on interracial relationships, Joane Nagel (2003:55) makes the academic argument that "negative images or accusations about . . . ethnic Others contribute to the creation of disreputable and toxic outgroups and can be used to justify their exclusion, repression, or extermination." In equally eloquent terms, a young man from Montana demonstrates just how the toxic images about which I have written here continue to impact the real lives of American Indians:

> And the hatred and the violence and the hurt, it's all mixed up in ideas of how Indian people are perceived, that they're savages, they don't know how to control themselves, or that they're violent. And in actuality, from history, it was the pioneers who were those things, not the Indians, not the Crow people. But that's continued, that attitude has continued, that Native people don't know how to behave or follow the rules, I mean from an Anglo perspective. And so then Anglos have this feeling they have the right to inflict violence without, you know . . . they just think they can do it.

Native and nonnative people enter each social interaction carrying with them the baggage that holds these stereotypical images. Racist discourse provides "a reservoir of procedural norms that not only tacitly inform routine activity but are also able to legitimate more purposive, explicitly racist practices" (S. Smith, 1989:150). It is within the cultural realm that we find the justifications for inequities, and for hate crime, for these processes are predicated on legitimating ideologies and images that mark the Other, and the boundaries between self and Other, in such a way as to normalize the corresponding inequities. As an example of the connection, consider the following:

> They do it, they give us a hard time 'cause they hate us. They think we're stupid and lazy, and that we get all these things from the government so we don't have to work. Sometimes I come out of the jobs place there, looking for work, and white guys start to shove me around, asking why do I come there? I don't really want to work. They think we can't do it, or will be drunk at work, anyway. One time, this guy got in my face and knocked me down. Part of me wanted to fight back, but I just got up and ran. I was scared 'cause there was some other guys with him. (Minnesota, male)

It is evident from this example how a body of discourse—"stupid, lazy, sponging" Indians—articulates the relations of superiority/inferiority, thereby establishing a hospitable environment for openly racist activity. Violence motivated by these preconceptions becomes an effort to prove one's whiteness—racial solidarity—relative to the defiled Other. It is a claim to superiority, which is meant to establish once and for all that the white perpetrator is not the Other. Rather, the perpetrator removes himself or herself from the victim group by engaging in violence directed against it; surely one would not seek to harm the self, only the Other.

Violence predicated on the outsider identity of the victim permits the perpetrator to reassert the normativity of the white American. It publicizes the perpetrator's message that he represents the ideal, and that people of color fail to meet the standard. The white offender is the permanent insider, the raced victim the permanent outsider, who must forever be reminded of his or her relative status. This is particularly evident in those cases where victims or potential victims are urged to "go back to the reservation." Here, the message is clear: that Indians don't belong, that they occupy an outsider status, despite their being aboriginal inhabitants of the land. Thus it is important to note the role hate crime plays in punishing those Others who have attempted to overstep their boundaries by assuming they, too, are worthy of first-class citizenship. This is especially evident at the localized points of contact where whites feel their identity, or safety, or sense of proprietorship threatened by unwelcome intrusions of people of color. Weis et al. uncovered such a sense of community loss in their interviews with white working-class men. These subjects expressed a "felt assault," a sense of "no longer belonging" in their own neighborhoods—sentiments they attributed to the influx of minorities "who[m] they clearly position as the other" (Weis, Proweller, and Centri, 1997:218). Similar perceptions underlie the violence associated with Native Americans who "wander off" the reservation—thereby crossing geographical boundaries—or who assert their rights—thereby crossing less tangible sociocultural boundaries. The following illustrates this point:

> For a while there, last year, the year before, I didn't want nothing to do with town. I didn't want to go in there. I always got in a fight—I didn't have to do nothing, just someone would ask me what I was doing off the res, how much beer I drank, what I was gonna steal, then they'd get to pushing me, and I, well, I'm not gonna stand there, huh? So I push back, and then we're rolling around. It ain't worth it. I stay here most times now. (Minnesota, male)

I will have much more to say about each of these particular variations of violence in subsequent chapters.

5
Contextualizing Native American Hate-Crime Victimization

> How do we, as a terminated people, understand the color of
> violence? We look at all the nonnative settlers and tourists
> around us and know we are subjugated in our own land, suffering
> landlessness and poverty, consigned by the American government
> to the periphery of our own country, to its prisons and shanties,
> to its welfare rolls, hospital wards, and graveyards.
> (Trask, 2004:9)

Trask demands of us that we see the violence that has oppressed and continues to oppress aboriginal peoples as embedded in an array of integrated practices. It shores up the historical and contemporary experience of exclusion and constraint, while at the same time it is a by-product of these. To be sure, Native Americans across the country continue to experience myriad and interrelated forms of economic, political, and social oppression. This is evident in practices ranging from negative cultural imaging, treaty abrogations, and violence. In fact, as pointed out in chapter 2, the images just discussed, and the practices of oppression to be explored in this chapter, provide the backdrop for a pattern of ongoing hate crime against Native Americans.

In the previous chapter, I detailed the enabling images that facilitate animosity, and thus violence, toward Native Americans. In this chapter, I explore the next three structural "faces of oppression" to which Young (1990; 1995) refers: exploitation, marginalization, and disempowerment. The discursive and structural conditions underpinning both historical and modern patterns of violence cannot be disaggregated. The former provide the rationale for the latter, and the effects of the latter seem to lend credence to the myths that have blurred Americans' ideas about Native Americans. I turn in this chapter toward the tangible strategies of colonial oppression, recognizing that "colonization introduced into the new continent forces far more destructive than ideas" (Sheehan, 1980: ix). Indeed, European and American colonial governments crafted an array of institutional practices intended to police and reaffirm the carefully constructed boundaries between colonized and colonizer. These patterns would not simply result in diminished sovereignty of Native American nations; colonization would also result in a narrowing of options even within the space that was newly created for Native American people.

Exploitation

Exploitation, from a traditional Marxist point of view, refers to the transfer of the product of labor power from the laborer to the capitalist. Taken further, it refers more generally to the appropriation of the powers and energies of one group by another, in such a way as to produce inequitable distributions of wealth, privilege, and benefits. In Young's (1990:73) words, it consists of a "steady process of the transfer of the results of one social group to benefit another . . . [It] enacts a structural and hierarchical relationship between social groups."

While typically understood in class terms, the processes associated with exploitation also apply to Native Americans as a people. Jack Forbes (1991) refers to the process of "proletarianization," as distinct from assimilation. By removing so many Native Americans from their land base, the colonizers "denationalized" Native Americans, reducing them to competitive individuals. The process also created the need to seek wage labor. This was not by accident. The slave labor of imported Africans was not sufficient to sustain the growing capitalist economy. Increasingly, Native Americans were forced into the labor market. Their land base and their traditional economies were so decimated that little alternative could be seen. Ironically, however, even the newly emerging employment opportunities were far from open to Native Americans. Along with other free people of color, they would be relegated to low-status work at best.

Historically, the labor of people of color, including American Indians, has been used only when necessary, and typically at very low skill and wage levels. Hence they have also tended to have elevated rates of unemployment. Job segregation, whereby people of color are relegated to menial and servile positions, has long been their lot. They are, in contrast, dramatically underrepresented in the professions. Indeed, the 2002 U.S. Census reveals that less than a quarter of all Native Americans are found in management and professional occupations, compared to over one-third of the general population. The situation is worse for some than for others, with members of the Lumbee and Navajo nations coming in at only about 20 percent each (United States Census Bureau, 2006:10).

Given that many of the people with whom I spoke lived on a reservation, there are a significant number in meaningful employment with the tribes—in chapter houses, senior centers, or community centers—and with state and federal agencies. In fact, nearly 20 percent of Native Americans are employed by federal, state, and local governments, compared to just under 15 percent of the general population (Housing Assistance Council, 2002). Yet even these fully employed workers share with the broader community a deep sense of frustration about the lack of good jobs in the area, and about the extent of discrimination exercised by nonnative employers in neighboring communities. As one Native man put it, "All the good jobs, we don't have a chance—no one wants to hire no Indians." Many of the limited jobs that *are* available are seasonal—in the tourist industry, or agriculture, for example. This is labor exploitation "at its best." Another Native American man from Arizona complained, "You'll see that around town as you talk to different people—they would use us as their front, in the summer months, and then once the tourists are gone, they're laid off, and so we're used that way. The people in town, the tourists, they like to see the Native Americans in the shop." Just as common, however, is to underemploy Native American workers—to keep them in low-skill, low-wage labor—again, an exploitive relationship with little in it for the workers. A higher proportion of Native Americans relative to the population are to be found in the lower wage sectors, such as service, maintenance, and agriculture (United States Census Bureau, 2006). This helps to explain the very strong perception in the communities visited that

> there's hardly any good jobs, you know? If there is, then make sure that her family, or her best friends' kids, make sure they get those jobs, and they line them up. And the only type of jobs they offer to Native Americans were janitorial jobs and things like that. So, I've seen it a lot of times, you know, it really bothered me when they did that. So you could only do what you can. (Utah, female)

Even within these sectors, there is a sense of further segregation by race, such that, as one Minnesota woman said, "They're in the back, they're in the kitchen. No, they're not the waiters—they're not the people you see when you walk into the restaurant. They're the garbage, you know? The cleaners. And you see that a lot."

Many of the communities I visited rely heavily on tourism for only a few months of the year. Consequently the types of jobs noted above are common and heavily dependent on the local Native American population. As one Native interviewee cited earlier reminds us, many people are employed only as long as they are needed, then left to languish for the rest of the year. From the perspective of employers, this is a perfectly acceptable practice; it is, to them, generous and beneficent. Where would these workers be otherwise? Participants seemed to believe that such treatment by employers is grounded in some of the persistent stereotypes noted in the previous chapter: they don't want to work; they would rather draw a welfare check; they're incapable of more demanding work. One woman from Minnesota sums up this sentiment:

> They think, Native Americans, that they're lazy, they won't work, they're not going to come to work, they always quit after the first few checks, which is a huge thing. You know, you get a lot of people like that. I can see their point of view, too. But at least give them a chance, let them work there, you know?

Even the self-directed labor of Native Americans is vulnerable to exploitation. In all of the regions visited, Native Americans are known for their artisan skills in jewelry making, pottery, basketry, etc. Where they are able to sell direct, as at the Native Americans for Community Action market near Flagstaff, Arizona, they and their families directly reap the profits of their labor. More often, however, they sell their arts and crafts to nonnative retailers and trading posts. It is here that exploitation reaches outlandish levels, as buyers pay a pittance, then charge shoppers a heavily inflated price, as in the following example:

> And then also, the jewelry business here, it works the same way, and a lot of these self-employed silversmiths and jewelry makers, they make their jewelry, but they never take into account the cost of the silver, the labor it took them to make it. And they'll be told, "Okay, I'll give you this because it's not worth that much," and they agree to it, some of them don't go around and ask why, and, all that work, and they get paid for so little . . . And then, it's six or seven times more than what they bought it for, or maybe even more, maybe even ten or twelve

times more. I worked for a business that used to do that, and I used to ask, "Why is it like this?" And they'd have all these signs set up saying that they're 50 percent off, and it's really not—it's 50 percent more! Yeah, and they still make all the money that they paid for it, they get all that back, plus 50 percent more than what they would have paid for it. I know that Gallup is like that, and that's probably why we have a lot of jewelry shops. And a lot of it is being exported, I guess, to different countries. And they make a lot of money. And it's like that everywhere in Gallup. (New Mexico, female)

Coinciding with the exploitive hiring and buying practices, Native Americans appear to be especially vulnerable to predatory lending practices, by which is meant "an unsuitable loan designed to exploit vulnerable and unsophisticated borrowers" (K. Smith, 2003:4). A 2003 report found that Native Americans were subject to an array of unscrupulous lending patterns, including charging more in interest and fees than is required to cover the potential added cost of lending to risky borrowers; abusive terms and conditions that lead borrowers to increased indebtedness; failure to take into account borrower's ability to repay the loan; and the violation of fair lending laws by targeting women and minorities (K. Smith, 2003:9–10). The report concluded that

> although the elderly are heavily targeted, first-time homebuyers are pursued as well as lower-income and minority community members, according to the Fannie Mae Foundation. Many tribes surveyed believe they are targeted because of the lack of financial lending institutions available on reservations and the difficulty in getting fair loans for mobile homes. These problems provide a breeding ground for predatory lenders and unfair practices. (K. Smith, 2003:21)

This observation would come as no surprise to many of those interviewed, who reported unfair and exploitive lending to be widespread among car dealers, mortgage and other similar lenders, mobile home retailers, and pawn shops. One woman catalogued virtually the whole array of questionable practices intended to separate her from her cash, including exorbitant interest rates—up to 50 percent on payday loans; high finance charges; unwillingness to clarify terms of loans or lease agreements; and excessive balloon payments. As the report cited above suggests, the elderly seem to be especially vulnerable, in part due to language difficulties, and in part due to the high-pressure tactics of the lenders. For example:

> They took advantage of my mom and dad, once again, and, you know, they had a vehicle, and they had this advertisement. I can't remember what it was, but they lured them into getting them a car. And then they repossessed the car, but they still say, you know, they send my mom bills for thirty thousand or something like that. I mean, it's not worth that much, if they have repossessed the car they should just say that's even, no more. But they keep adding interest and all this other stuff where they say they owe. Maybe it's the same rate, too, 300 percent by the time they get through paying it. (Utah, female)

The collective impact of these practices is to reinforce the impoverishment of the local Native American communities. Low wages, combined with unsavory purchase and loan practices, hinders their ability to improve their lot through savings, for example. Added to this is the debilitating impact of the lengthy history of resource exploitation (Churchill, 1992; Osborne, 1995). American Indians have lost over 95 percent of their land base. What is left is indeed resource rich. However, consecutive abrogations of treaty rights to mineral resources, water, and fishing (Fixico, 1998) have all but ceded control of such resources to governments, corporations, and other private interests at the expense of Native economies. Even on the local level, individual land owners feel cheated out of full market value for leased land:

> Yeah, yeah, that is the hard one, is the different resources, because here on the Crow reservation, the land leasing, purchasing, too, but primarily leasing, has been so that there's no way that anybody's going to be able to change it. So the leasing of land, which is how ranchers and farmers make their money, it's so low on the reservation, it's not even market value. Off reservation for a rancher, he gets charged fourteen dollars in the spring, and on the reservation it's five dollars, so it's not even close to fair market value. (Montana, male)

In these cases, the land itself is at issue. More typically, however, it is what the land offers up in terms of resources that causes conflict, generally at the expense of American Indian communities. Because of the exploitation of mineral resources in the Upper Midwest, for example, the Ojibwe people have faced greater impoverishment, while several generations of East Coast copper and iron mining companies were enriched. Also set in motion were the great mining and lumber booms that ultimately fizzled out, leaving large portions of the Lake Superior region in a severe economic depression that continues to this day (Gedicks, 1991).

In retrospect, the historical relationship that evolved between colonizer and colonized underlies the exploitation that is occurring today. American Indian tribes believe in a strong sense of balance. Before the first Europeans came, a massive American Indian land base existed. The trees, earth, and the sense and sight of the environment itself influenced the intellect and thinking process of the Indians in creating the notion of balance. This precarious balance still exists, and the relationship between plants and animals, the air, water, wind, and earth, are all equally and evenly placed within the whole. For many American Indians even today, the way of life revolves around the environment. Humans do not, and indeed cannot, own the elements of nature if a healthy balance is to be maintained. Rather, only what is necessary to survive is taken from the earth.

This is very much in contrast to, first, European, and then, American land utilization practices, which were often imposed on the Ojibwe through inequitable treaties. Again, we see the conflict in values, this time manifest in exploitive Western practices. Fixico (1998:136) highlights the implications of the competing presence of "the driving forces of two very different cultures, two incongruent sets of values and two divergent perspectives on the same geographical area. Both factions want the land [or its resources]—one as a source of valuable natural resources and the other as a spiritual center, a link to the understanding of life."

The irony, of course, is that some nonnatives accuse Native Americans of hyperexploiting resources. Hysteria has been constructed by anti-Indian groups over what they consider to be outdated Indian treaties and misuse of resources. Angry protestors, sports fishermen, those in the tourist industry, the state of Wisconsin, and the multinational corporate giants would like to see the dissolution of treaties, without realizing the benefit treaties have for all people. The anti-Indian groups fail to realize that treaties that protect hunting, fishing, and gathering also protect the environment. What good is the treaty right to spearfish if the waters and fish are forever poisoned by the environmentally destructive process of mining? The bottom line is that treaties preserve the land and resources for everyone.

However, sustainability has usually taken a backseat when set against the economics of capitalism in our industrial society, and the anti-Indian movement has historically been linked to the economic expansionary needs of American capitalism. As argued in chapter 3, when the dominant Euroamerican society needed land and raw materials for expansion, Indians were defined as a problem or a threat, and their lands and resources were taken. Now, having been left with the land nobody else wanted, it turns out that some of the last remaining energy and mineral resources are located on Indian lands or on off-reservation lands in the ceded territory of Wisconsin. The hysteria generated by anti-Indian groups is grounded precisely in this tendency to imagine the Ojibwe as the culprits rather than as protectors of the land. This sentiment is reflected in the following observation made by an Ojibwe man from Wisconsin who had been active in the spearfishing conflicts:

> That hierarchy of racism is still there . . . We've never gotten an apology from America for what they've done to our people and to our lands. Every other ethnic group has today—Japanese, blacks. We helped America since when they first came here; we continue to. We try to fish and hunt according to old traditions that are meant to keep the earth and its creatures healthy. We try to teach others, too. But then we get blamed for the opposite. It's the Sunday fishermen and the fishing business and the mines that have hurt our lakes. They take, take, take, and then blame us.

There are those in Native American communities who see the "rape of the land" itself as a heinous form of violence (A. Smith, 2005):

> Well, you see how that violence transfers on all these levels. When I talk about the land, it's not as clean and simple as somebody getting beat up, or somebody getting killed. It cuts a lot of wings, and, you know, it's the land, it's the land that gives us our identity, our sense of being, our sense of belonging, our sense of place. And when you radically alter that landscape, what do you become? Some of those areas down there, it's almost like a desert in terms of the things that we need. Yeah, kinda like those little bitty Coppell trees [an invasive plant] as big as your thumb, coming up all over the place, you know, they're two feet apart, and you can hardly walk through it. (Minnesota, male)

The extent to which this conflict over relationship to the land underlies contemporary violence will be explored in detail in the next chapter. For now, suffice it to say that attempts to assert treaty rights in the face of ruinous exploitation of land and resources have been at the heart of a great deal of recent anti-Indian hate crime.

Marginalization

Related to the exploitation of American Indians and their lands is the marginalization of Native Americans—"expulsion from useful participation in social life" (Young, 1995:77). As such, it restricts the capacities and opportunities of an entire group of people in ways that leave them, quite literally, on the political, economic, and social fringes. This marginalization is a sort of invisibility. Certainly, a glance at the local newspapers in the communities I visited gave very little indication that American Indians lived in the area. Rather, American Indian issues were absent, to be found only in local, regional, or national Native media outlets but not in mainstream newspapers. Of course, there were exceptions. The daily Flagstaff, Arizona, newspaper, for example, regularly featured Native American issues, often devoting lengthy multiple-part special sections to problems or successes in Indian Country. For the most part, though,

> from even the perspective of public relations, in terms of newspapers and so forth, I see very little written up on Native Americans specifically here, Navajos and Utes, no place in the community. Plus the commercial outlets don't carry, for example the *Navajo Times*. One has to travel distances to get a copy of the *Navajo Times*. (Utah, male)

This invisibility carries over into other areas as well. Most prominent, perhaps, is the perception that Native Americans receive disparate service in stores and other businesses. Here, too, they feel as if they must be blending into the background:

> To give an example, two years ago when I went in there, I stayed in line, they had two lines going up to the counter. So I'm standing there, waiting to get served, and all of a sudden . . . when I got up there, she kind of shifted over to the other one and said, "Who's next?" And I go, "Hey, what about me?" "Oh, I didn't see you"—like that. And I said, "Christ, am I skinny standing sideways, or whatever, you can't see me?" "Oh, I'm sorry." (Minnesota, male)

Even those on the other side of the counter—service providers, rather than customers—must often deal with rebuffs from clients who would rather not deal with one of "them," but rather, one of "us." Several of those interviewed spoke of their experiences with clients who decided they would rather wait longer or come back later, rather than be assisted by a Native American. Discrimination, clearly, affects those who provide services as much as those seeking them:

> And before my other co-worker, before she came, there was another Anglo in there, and the majority of her cases were Anglos, and a lot of times they would call to make appointments, they'd either come in or call by the phone, and they would say, "I want to make an appointment with the white one." Or, "I really don't want to be served by the Indian." I just make a joke out of it, and that really ticks them off. It's still like that. (Arizona, female)

This story highlights but one way in which the work environment can promote the marginality of workers. Here, clients selectively preclude Native Americans from being able to do their job; they resist the relatively powerful position represented by the human services industry in particular. This appeared to be a particular problem when white people were forced to ask an American Indian for assistance, as in counseling or advising work.

There are many other ways in which Native Americans experience exclusionary processes in the context of labor. In the previous section on exploitation, I referred to employment discrimination. This comes into play in reinforcing the marginality of Native Americans as well. Because of the lack of viable employment opportunities for Native Americans, their participation rate lags behind that of the general population. For all men and all women, the participation rates are 70.7 percent and 57.5 percent, respectively; for Native American men and women, they are 65.6 percent and 56.8 percent, respectively. However, this occludes dramatic differences between Native American communities, in that labor-force participation rates drop below 50 percent among such Indian nations as the Navajo (United States Census Bureau, 2006). Together, patterns of underemployment and unemployment place Native Americans at the very fringes of the economy, such that Native Americans, more than any other racial or ethnic group, live in poverty (see table). Additionally, median incomes of Native American households are also substantially lower than other groups, with the exception of African Americans (see table). By virtue of their chronic unemployment and meager incomes, Native Americans remain economically parceled off from the

Table Poverty Levels (1999)† and Median Family Incomes (2004)‡ by Race and Hispanic Origin

	Number (in thousands) below Poverty Line (%)	Median Income (in dollars)
All races	33,900 (12.4)	44,389
White	18,848 (9.1)	46,697
Black	8,146 (24.9)	30,134
American Indian and Alaska Native	608 (25.7)	32,866
Asian	1,257 (12.6)	57,518
Native Hawaiian and Other Pacific Islander	65 (17.7)	51,687
Hispanic or Latino	7,798 (22.6)	34,241

†U.S. Census Bureau, 2006
‡U.S. Census Bureau, 2005

mainstream, "unable to exercise capacities in socially defined and recognized ways" (Young, 1995:77). This serves to reinforce those stereotypes of lazy, incapable Indians. This is the worst form of victim blaming, when those who are structurally excluded are held accountable for the lack of opportunities available to them. That Native people are often left with few options but to seek social assistance similarly reproduces the cycle of dependency, for which they are also blamed. A woman from Montana describes Native Americans' limited access to jobs at one of the northern region's largest employers:

> We have Glacier National Park, it has a large number of jobs because of the different properties they own. Ten major properties on and off the reservation that surrounds Glacier Park. So the numbers of employees they could hire through their commissaries, 'cause they

get commission-type of contracts with individuals. So as far as the hiring "piece" here, tribes in Montana and throughout the United States have that office, employment office, so the hiring here is . . . We have a high number of people unemployed, so why are you hiring people from university systems, Connecticut, New York, I mean, across the country, when you can look at your own local base here . . . And so what has happened, it's just now, in the last three to five years, where they have been hiring more local individuals. It's very seasonal, but still it's . . . I mean, not everybody can be firefighters here, even though that's preferred.

The economics of marginalization are facilitated by the legacy of the reservation system. For the one-third of Native Americans living on the reservations, the geopolitical boundaries have contributed to their economic isolation. As argued in chapter 3, more so than other minority groups, American Indians have even been geographically marginalized, first through westward expulsion, and subsequently by forced relocation onto the reservations (Stiffarm and Lane, 1992). Over the course of the nineteenth century, the United States government entered into more than 600 land treaties with Indian nations, which typically ceded all but the least arable land. Over time, much of the ceded territory was also lost through treaty abrogation, with the result that by the close of that century the American Indian land base had shrunk to less than 5 percent of their territory within what is now the United States (Washburn, 1995), conditions about which Native Americans interviewed had much to say.

> What they did back in the time of the Cochises and the Crazy Horses, that's no different than what they're doing to us today, in other ways—trying to keep us quiet, keep us separate. The give ya just enough to survive—sometimes not even that. Look at Rosebud, look at the land where you are, on Navajo land—they're all still struggling. (Wisconsin, male)

> We're put in parks, like the animals, you know, in the Interior Department. We're put to one side, behind fences, on reservations, like the deer and the geese. Can't they find us another category to put our nation? (Utah, male)

As Razack (2005) says, "Place is race," and Native Americans' place since the mid-1800s has been, in part, on the reservations. "Ghettoization" has plagued Native Americans as much as it has African Americans, yet in this context, the ghetto is usually rural. As of the 2000 census, just under two million American Indians lived in urban areas, while half as many resided on largely rural reservations; indeed, 70 percent of those living on reservations lived in rural communities (Taylor and Kalt, 2005; United States Census Bureau, 2006). Yet these numbers cannot be taken at face value, since those living off-reservation in urban areas often migrate back to reservations for varied lengths of time (Fixico, 2000). Thus part of their lives are also lived in more remote areas. Interestingly, "the relative proportions that lived in urban and rural settings were roughly inverted from the United States average" (Taylor and Kalt, 2005:4). The employment restrictions noted above are in large part attributable to this geographic isolation.

It is important to emphasize that segregation did not occur naturally, of its own accord, out of the relationship between white and nonwhite populations and cultures. Razack (2005) writes that we like to believe that urban ghettoes and rural reservations evolved organically. Nothing could be further from the truth, given that the geography of race was, in fact, the product of violent repression by the white community (Wachtel, 1999:222; see also Feagin, 2001:60). As noted previously, black ghettoes were created, in part, as zones of safety, as defenses against collective assaults on blacks migrating to northern cities for work. So, too, were Native American reservations outgrowths of white violence, though in a slightly different, even more unnatural way. It might be said that these were America's first "planned" communities, in that land was reserved for subsequent American Indian inhabitants. But they were not, for the most part, voluntary inhabitants. On the contrary, they were forced— again, by military might and white settlers—onto the reservation land. The violence in this case was purposeful, a conscious exercise of disempowerment and isolation. And the violence had its intended effect of moving the nonwhite threat into distinct and isolated communities.

Ironically, for many Native Americans, the reservations do not represent the margin but rather the center. As I discuss in much greater detail in chapter 7, many return to or remain on the reservation as a means of finding their place. They are at once sites of despair and sites of hope, of oppression and of resistance. Thus these practices of geographic marginalization have had ambiguous effects. It is true that Native Americans were forced onto reservation lands—sometimes lands that had not previously been part of their territory, sometimes small corners of their original land base. As demoralizing as it must have been for Native people to lose so much land, the reservation system had its advantages. It allowed a measure of autonomy and control of albeit diminished pockets of land, as opposed to being forcibly assimilated on lands they could no longer claim as their own. As noted before, the reservation would come to represent a safe haven to which Native Americans could return, whether physically or spiritually. As Valaskakis (2005:114), contends, "However limited in area or resources, these territories—for which the Ojibwe word means 'leftovers'—are homelands for Native people, for whom identifying other Native people begins with the [question,] Where are you from?"

The tendency to physically and economically marginalize indigenous peoples is accompanied by social marginalization. The historical separation of Indian from non-Indian leaves a legacy of segregation, in which the two cultures are held apart. Through violence, the threat of violence, or even through the malevolent gaze, Native Americans are daily reminded that there are places where they are not welcome. The historical legacy of colonialism persists in the social and physical isolation experienced by so many residents of these rural enclaves. And just as the initial establishment of the reservations was facilitated through state and popular violence, so, too, does the contemporary reality of racialized violence keep reservation Indians in their place. I will return to this theme in chapter 7.

Disempowerment

Marginality facilitates powerlessness. By its very tendency to exclude, it renders Native Americans impotent. Moreover, powerlessness is both an outcome of other forms of oppression and independent in its internal dynamics. It represents both exclusion from participation in the wider society, as well as restrictions on autonomy and on decision-making capacities. Poupart (2002:152) acknowledges the reality of powerlessness for contemporary American Indian tribes—along with its link to systemic violence:

> Today, American Indian Nations remain depressed economically, politically, and socially. The disempowerment of Nations and the establishment of the federal trust relationship—making them wards

of the federal government—placed Indian Nations in a complicated position of dependency upon their oppressors. This relationship promotes ongoing genocide.

The imposition of this relationship by the federal government, in particular, has weakened Native American rights to exercise self-determination (Robbins, 1992; Snyder-Joy, 1996). The processes of colonization represented a major factor in the disempowerment of Native Americans, since it is more than just a convenient economic domination of one people by another. Colonization continues to undermine the political, military, social, psychocultural, values, law and order, and knowledge bases of the colonized, while imposing the values and culture of the colonizer.

This is a natural outgrowth of the long-lived perception of American Indians as unable to govern themselves. Paternalism—and greed for land—demanded that they be regulated for their own good. Never mind the rich political traditions and the legacy of democratic process that informed many precontact communities. In fact, this is something that was formally recognized by eighteenth-century philosophers and state builders. The latter adapted principles of the Iroquois Confederacy into the United States Constitution. Thus early on, the federal government recognized American Indian nations' sovereignty. It is only in this context that treaties could be brokered between parties. Nonetheless, this respect for Native American traditions would not last long. Already, by the 1830s, Jackson would be among the first U.S. presidents to weaken the status of recognized Indian nations (Takaki, 1994). In part, this was accomplished by refusing to intervene when states impinged on Indian rights and land. He would readily agree to the terms suggested in a letter to him from General John Coffee of Georgia:

> Deprive the chiefs of the power they now possess, take from them their own code of laws, and reduce them to plain citizenship . . . and they will soon determine to move, and then there will be no difficulty in getting the poor Indians to give their consent. All this will be done by the State of Georgia if the United States do not interfere with her law. (cited in Takaki, 1994:61)

Over time, the federal government (and individual states) would make successive efforts to disempower tribal communities. One of the most intrusive of these actions was the unilateral introduction in 1953 of Public Law 280. Initially this bill gave five states civil and criminal jurisdiction over Indian lands; nine more states would be added later. Together, these became the fourteen states with the largest concentrations of Native Americans. This bill, and others like it, denied tribes the right to govern themselves.

Even at the relatively mundane level of formal politics, Native Americans find themselves out of the loop. Of course, they manage internal tribal politics. But even this has been affected by the relationship of tribes to government—federal, state, and local. To the extent that surrounding municipalities have jurisdiction over Native American lands, tribes' ability to define their own destiny is largely circumscribed. This, too, is an artifact of historical colonialism, which has cumulatively reined in the leverage of sovereign Indian nations. Subsequent treaty abrogations and federal legislation have conspired to ensure that Indian nations have minimal autonomous status. Rather than recognizing them as sovereign states, the federal government nurtures a dependent status, reducing American Indian states to the level of county government. In fact, it often goes beyond this, to the extent that adjoining counties and municipalities can infringe on the sovereignty of Native lands. Consequently, Indian nations are forced into a position of having to accede to the structural, often legal constraints imposed by external bodies.

One potential response to this might have been to engage in the politics of surrounding communities, to wrestle some modicum of control through the unavoidable machinery of local politics. However, when it comes to off-reservation politics, American Indians have yet to make significant inroads. There have ever been only three Native American U.S. senators: Charles Curtis (R-Kansas), a Kaw who served from 1907 to 1913, and again from 1915 to 1929; Robert Owen (D-Oklahoma), a Cherokee who served from 1907 to 1925; and most recently, Ben Nighthorse Campbell (R-Colorado), a Northern Cheyenne who served from 1993 to 2005. Currently, there is but one Native American in the House of Representatives. The Native community fares better at the state level, where most western states generally have some American Indian representation.

At the level of local politics, there is a mixed bag. Even in border towns there is no consistent pattern to Native American representation. People interviewed had quite different perceptions of the level of involvement in their communities, depending on their location, as in the following observations from two Native American women, the first in Utah, the second in Arizona:

> We have no representation whatsoever, but I think there's two seats that are open and we're going to try to push two Native Americans in there if we can, if we can get, you know, all the Navajo people together so we can support the two people that will be running. And I think we'll be successful because, like I said, about half of them are Native American, so we should have a say in some of the things that are being done in the city council.

> No, there's no representation. I don't know why they don't run, but we do have a Native American judge on the judicial system, but I don't know how much good he's doing . . . We have one [police officer], we have a Native American highway patrolman, all he does is give tickets to all the Navajos.

The second statement raises the important issue of law enforcement, and the role that officers might play in empowering or disempowering a community. I have argued elsewhere (Perry, 2006) that police enhance the vulnerability of Native Americans by the dual processes of over- and underpolicing. The latter is especially relevant in thinking about the disempowerment of Native Americans, which is furthered by governments, especially law enforcement agencies, that do not take their concerns seriously. Many of those interviewed noted the extent to which the state plays an active role in maintaining the subordinate place of Native Americans in Wisconsin. Such a perception is not surprising in light of the comments of one Wisconsin police officer:

> It [hate crime] isn't here. I've lived here and worked here or lived outside the reservation, worked inside the reservation . . . The majority of people just want to get along. Go about their business, live their lives, don't want any problems, and they won't do anything of a prejudice nature, that wouldn't be considered a hate crime because they wouldn't want to get involved in something like that. They're overall just good law-abiding citizens, there are just a few bad apples that love to instigate a little problem and looking for a scapegoat in life, and it is always easy to blame one race no matter which race it is. Blaming another for some type of problem.

Such declarations fly in the face of the experiences described so candidly by people in all of the communities I visited. Such blindness—willful or otherwise—to the plight of the people they are intended to serve speaks volumes about how police view Native American communities. Denial of the problem absolves them of the responsibility of confronting it. Where victimization does not occur, where it is merely imagined by wannabe victims, police can and do turn a blind eye to the violence perpetrated against Native Americans. This was quite evident in the Upper Midwest, during the spearfishing conflicts:

> My husband was arrested along with another man for holding up the Plains Indian flag at a boat landing. Well, we forgot to tell you the whole point of that story, which is: the protestors had ordered the police to arrest them. And as it turned out, they had them in a back of a squad car, and there was frantic radio communication back and forth to try to find something to charge them with. They ended up successfully suing the county and various law enforcement entities. *And* a friend and treaty-rights supporter was also arrested at a joint PARR/STA rally at Torpy Park in Minocqua for holding up a sign reading People Already Racist (and) Radical (PARR), and we were there, and the PARR speakers actually ordered the law enforcement to arrest her even though all she was doing was silently standing there holding up a sign. And the police, at PARR's direction, did arrest her. We passed the hat and got money to bail her out. The main points are that in those times the police were actually being manipulated by the anti-Indian groups. And very openly, as the man who called for her arrest did so by microphone from a stage. (Wisconsin, female)

Often, lack of response by police is shaped by the denial of any threat to the community. The reasoning goes, where there is no violence, there can be no reason for action.

> You don't want to call the police or make an issue of it. They play down how serious the violence is, how much there is—unless it's Indians hurting whites. They see the cases one at a time if at all, so they won't make the connections. The cases aren't related; it's not about discrimination, they say. They won't admit that Indians get hurt more. (Montana, male)

This appears to hold true across the spectrum of violence. That is, police are thought to be as unresponsive to minor problems, such as automobile accidents or harassment, as they are to much more serious threats to physical safety. The former is apparent in the observations that follow, that police would, for example, take their time responding to traffic accidents. Even more disturbing, however, is the contention that they do not take violent victimization seriously, either. Again, there was a widespread belief that police were less than thorough in investigating violent deaths and homicides of Native American victims. Two women who were interviewed together recited a litany of uninvestigated or underinvestigated deaths in the Northern Plains, stating, "It's nothing new. Since first contact, dead Indians haven't drawn much attention." The concrete experiences of Native Americans interviewed confirm these perceptions. Many Native Americans reported a lack of police intervention, even in the face of imminent danger. One Ojibwe man from Minnesota told the story of being held at gunpoint. His wife called the county sheriff's office, and within twenty minutes an officer was on the scene. However,

> he looks at the situation, he looks at this dude standing there holding a shotgun, and I'm standing in one spot, because I don't want to move, and he's drunk, and the county cop looks at it and says, "I don't have any jurisdiction here," and gets in his car and drives away. And he was getting madder, he wasn't cooling off, he was getting more and more worked up as this thing was unfolding, and so as this thing went on and on and on, she finally said, "Okay." We had reservation officers, tribal game wardens. She said, "I'll go see if I can get one of them up here." I couldn't believe it. I batted zero that day, because he walked up, or drove up, he had his uniform, he had his gun, he had his truck, he had the full thing. He looked at it and said, "This is not my jurisdiction." And he went on his way. Finally, the guy, this was going on for like an hour and a half or two hours, and I was, "Oh man!" Finally I think the guy had to take a leak or something . . . "Not my jurisdiction." I couldn't believe, I was gonna die, and that's all they could say!

In this case, the failure of law enforcement to intervene in events unfolding before their very eyes could easily have had fatal consequences for the person involved. In the eyes of Native Americans, the willingness or unwillingness of police to take such a risk signals the relative worth of American Indian lives.

The malign neglect of Native American victims leaves communities vulnerable, cutting off access to the protections afforded nonnative victims of crime. These negligent practices extend a powerful message that justifies the violent marginalization of Native Americans. They signal to perpetrators, criminal justice personnel, and the rest of society that anti-Indian violence will not be punished. As I will discuss at greater length in the following chapter, while it is bad enough that law enforcement condones victimization by inaction, in some cases they step further over that line, actively facilitating violence by word and deed, and engaging in racist violence themselves.

In chapters 3 and 4, and here in chapter 5, I have traced the broad outlines of a legacy of the interconnected patterns of colonialism and racism. Both of these are the foundations of modern-day forms of violence perpetrated against Native Americans. Consequently, hate crime against Native Americans can be seen through the two separate though related lenses of racism and colonialism—sometimes simultaneously, sometimes discretely.

I would argue that most perpetrators of anti-Indian violence are acting/reacting on the basis of stereotypes or some other nebulous idea of how Native Americans ought to act, or are thought to act. Most are not sophisticated enough to put these images in the context of questions of Native American sovereignty. Thus a great deal of the hate crime perpetrated against Native American people is, in fact, grounded in the racialized images and patterns noted in chapters 4 and 5. They are victims of racialized violence informed by cultural images of lazy or drunken Indians. It has little to do with their status as a rights-bearing collective.

However, there is simultaneously a subset of violence that is a direct descendent of the colonialist violence highlighted in chapter 3. For those within or inspired by the anti-Indian movement that has been active in the Pacific Northwest and the Great Lakes region, violence is explicitly connected to Native American assertions of sovereignty. Reactionary violence in the face of Native land claims, or other related demands for the recognition of sovereign rights, is an all-too-common reality. This is a reflection of the refusal of Native American communities to be wholly defeated. Historical practices aimed at eradication or assimilation have weakened but not destroyed Native American peoples. Many such communities retain significant measures of autonomy, through local, regional, and national campaigns of self-assertion. Tribal governments thrive; individual nations as well as broader coalitions assert treaty rights, resist treaty abrogations, and attempt to extend their land bases. As chapter 7 will explore in detail, the reactionary violence to these efforts often has the contradictory effect of hardening the resolve of Native American activists.

6
The Forgotten Victims
Hate Crimes against Native Americans

The historical and contemporary patterns described in the preceding chapters have cultivated an environment that leaves Native Americans vulnerable to ongoing violence. Drawing again on Young (1990; 1995), I argue that the largely derogatory images of Native Americans, along with their relatively disadvantaged structural position, leaves them in a position of vulnerability. It is the context of hate crimes that "makes them possible and even acceptable. What makes violence a phenomenon of social injustice and not merely an individual moral wrong is its systemic character, its existence as a social practice, its legitimacy" (Young, 1995:83). As we will see in this chapter, hate crime also reinforces these patterns of exclusion and oppression.

In the two previous chapters, I referred to the many instances of all the components of oppression noted earlier. All are apparent from the visible socioeconomics of the communities I visited—from archival materials, from newspaper and TV news stories, and from the stories of the people who live there. Myriad forms of exploitation are evident (e.g., exploitation of Native American craftspeople), as are practices that constitute cultural imperialism (e.g., racial slurs, the absence of American Indians in school curricula). However, I was especially struck by the empirical validity of the conceptual observation that Native Americans live with the "daily knowledge . . . that they are *liable* to violation, solely on account of their group identity" (Young, 1995:83). In other words, the American Indians who spoke with me reported a lifetime's worth of microaggressions, "a term used to describe racial assaults, subtle, stunning, often automatic and non-verbal exchanges which are 'put-downs' of Blacks by Whites," and one might say, of Native Americans (Russell, 1998:138).

What I am referring to here are the everyday acts of omission and commission that remind minority group members of their place. These often include discriminatory acts by criminal justice representatives—racial profiling or disparate sentencing, for example. But they also include the daily onslaught of thoughtless acts by laypeople—the use of insulting labels and language; threats against those "in the wrong place"; violence against those seen to be crossing inappropriate social or political or even geographical boundaries. Writer and activist bell hooks (1995:15) attests to the violent potential inherent in the game of racial accountability. She observes that the daily violence experienced by so many black people

> is necessary for the maintenance of racial difference. Indeed, if black people have not learned our place as second-class citizens through educational institutions, we learn it by the daily assaults perpetuated by white offenders on our bodies and beings that we feel but rarely publicly protest or name . . . Most black folks believe that if they do not conform to white dominated standards of acceptable behavior they will not survive.

As many Native American or black or Asian or Latino people know, the white gaze is upon them, judging them not only against their own whiteness but also against those imposed standards to which hooks refers. Hate crime, then, is but one mechanism along the continuum of micro-aggressions that underlie the contemporary racial hierarchy that seeks to maintain the relative disempowerment of Native Americans and other racial minorities.

Over a period of four years, I spent many hours, many days, in fact, listening to stories that had previously gone largely untold. I have provided an outlet for voices long silenced by inhibitions ranging from fear of violence, to forms of personal denial, to perceptions of official apathy. I am speaking here of stories of racist victimization experienced by Native Americans. My observations across venues as diverse as Northern Wisconsin and Northern Arizona have revealed some remarkably consistent patterns of experiences and perceptions. This chapter begins to tell those stories. In so doing, I also attempt to put the violence in the context of the enabling conditions described in chapters 4 and 5. That is, I draw the links between the images and the structural constraints, and hate crime.

The Continuum of Violence

Across state and tribal lines, it is distressingly clear that racial violence and harassment are normative parts of the everyday experience of

Native Americans. Of the nearly three hundred Native Americans who were interviewed, the majority had either themselves been victims or knew of someone close to them who had been a victim of some form of hate crime, ranging from verbal harassment, to pushing and shoving, to brutal assaults with knives and lighter fluid. By far the most common incidents were various types of name-calling and verbal harassment on the street and in commercial establishments.

> You can go to certain places and they will get you there. "What the hell you doing here?" "Why aren't you on the res?" "Dirty Indians shouldn't be in here." The one place if I went down there today they would be all shitty is the Diary Queen at Minocqua. The guy, the manager's really nice every time, he's nice, he's helpful, he's truthful. But it is the people that work there. They're just shitty there. They want to be sure that when they hand you something you don't touch their skin, like, "Oh my god, I've got cooties." That gets kinda sickening. Feel sorry for them. (Wisconsin, male)

This is very much in line with what we know generally about the nature and distribution of hate crime. It does tend to be largely restricted to offenses at the lower end of the spectrum, what might more properly be called bias "incidents," rather than bias crimes. But that does not make them any less significant. We have learned from the literature on violence against women, for example, that the daily onslaught of verbal abuse has far-reaching consequences for the victim. The same can be said of racial harassment, to the extent that it is also an almost daily occurrence in many communities.

This is not to say that extreme violence is unheard of. There were also a number of cases at the other end of the spectrum. Among the most vicious attacks were two cases in which perpetrators bit their victims. In one of these, a small piece of the victim's ear was bitten off; in the other, the tip of the victim's tongue. In one community, several people shared the same story of a local Native American man who had been set on fire with lighter fluid.

The most prolonged and vicious patterns of extreme violence, however, occurred at the Wisconsin boat landings in the 1990s, during the spearfishing conflicts. Native people who participated in this activism shared some remarkable tales of their experiences. Attackers fired shots, lobbed rocks and pipe bombs at them, and created dangerous waves that rocked their boats while they were out on the water. Such violence, among the most extreme, highlights the intensity of the response to Native Americans' assertions of sovereignty. I will return to this theme of reactionary violence later in the chapter.

Between these two extremes, however, there are endless examples of other types of physical and property offenses. One category I had not anticipated had to do with property crimes in the ranching communities of Montana. Several people interviewed mentioned the common acts of vandalism and sabotage that occurred when white ranchers lost their lease on Native-owned land. Some of these leases had been for fifty years or more. When the current Native owners refused to renew the lease—often so they could ranch the land themselves or offer the lease to other Native American ranchers—the white ranchers became incensed. Apparently it was not uncommon for them to retaliate by damaging the new lessee's farm equipment, or even to set the fields on fire, as in the following example:

> I had that—them white ranchers didn't like me. I got my lease back, and I planted that one big field. The neighbor there called me one night, he said I better get there, my field was on fire. He called in the fire but said I need to go there. By the time the fire truck came, half that field was gone. I know it was that rancher. He had my lease last year, I didn't give it back. He was pissed off, told me it was his land, he'd worked it, he made it good. I didn't know how to grow anything, all of that. I know he done it, 'cause he was pissed off, you know. (Montana, male)

This particular case also brings to light the persistence of the long-standing perception that Native Americans have no right to the land because they don't know how to exploit it.

Crimes of physical violence were also commonplace. Virtually without exception, high schools were described as very unwelcoming and often dangerous places for Native American youth:

> We see a lot of this, it's about every day. Not only just because of what happened to my son, but the years before, even when his mother was going to school there, it was the same way. They've always been targets, those kids, our kids. White kids—even teachers—don't think [anything] about hitting them, slapping them. Kids are beating them up in the school yard. My wife had that and my kids get that—they

don't want to go over to that school. They don't want to face all that
stuff. (Minnesota, male)

Nonviolent and violent forms of oppression coalesce to make schools
threatening places for some Native American students. Here, the
expressed racism of fellow students and faculty alike can take the tangible form of racial harassment and violence—that is, hate crime. The
experiences seem to indicate that ethnoviolence is, in fact, embedded
in broader practices and perceptions associated with oppression. Comments from other students, even from faculty, send the message to students that they do not belong on campus, thereby further alienating
and marginalizing Native American students. Occasionally this is quite
explicit, as when students are admonished to "go back to the reservation." More frequently, it is implicit in the assertions and subtler expressions that Native Americans are somehow intellectually inferior and
therefore do not belong in school for that reason.

Yet it is not only youth who are subject to violence and harassment:

We were just getting there and were getting our chair or our table
ready, and these guys got up and they were loud and drinking, you
know, and mouthy. They got up, and as they were leaving the one guy
put his coat on and punched my mom in the back, and she went fly-
ing. "What the fuck you doing on the floor? What the hell is the matter with you? Drunk, of course." And they were acting like . . . "What,
what? We weren't doing nothing." (Wisconsin, male)

This particular example is interesting for a number of reasons. First, it
shows that age is no barrier to the likelihood of victimization. The victim in this case was an elderly woman. It also draws on the stereotype of
the drunken Indian to distance the perpetrators from their acts—*they*
were not the guilty ones. In fact, they did nothing to contribute to the
"drunk" falling down. Additionally, however, it highlights the intent of
the violence: to keep these Native Americans out of the way of white
people; to keep them out of "our" places of business.

Other examples abound. Many Native Americans shared memories
of their own victimization, or that of friends and family members. And,
as with youth in schools, adult victimization is commonly predicated on
the sorts of stereotypes noted in chapter 4. Most typical is the exploitation of the stereotype of the drunken Indian to justify the abuse meted
out. Consequently, the age-old practice of "rolling drunken Indians" is

alive and well in Indian Country (see also Barker, 1992). Several dramatic illustrations were provided by participants, of which the following was typical:

> It's bad here, I know from myself that it is. Sometimes—I don't live in town—and I come in and I have some drinks and I can't get home. So I, a lot of us, we go to the park when it's warm and we can't go home. It's bad all the time. These white boys, they come all the time, they give us a bad time, threaten us, push us around. My eye, I can't hardly see anything 'cause of that one time. I'm there, and I'm standing around, and they come—they just pushed me around some, then really hard, and I fell down. Then they started kicking me, man, I was yelling "Stop, stop!" and they kept going, laughing, calling me "stupid drunk Indian. Go back to the res. We don't want you here." I was so scared, and they really messed me up. The one kid, he hit me in the eye two or three times. I can't hardly see now. It's bad here. (Arizona, male)

From this brief overview, it is apparent that hate crime against Native Americans runs the gamut, from relatively benign acts of harassment to vicious physical assaults. And as many of the previous illustrations suggest, there is a widespread perception that the violence is ordinary, rather than extraordinary: that it comes to be seen as a normal part of life in Indian Country.

The Normativity of Violence

> The Crow people have it in their heart that just by walking down the street, or seeing him in the wrong place, if they're alone especially and don't know anyone, or if they've been drinking or whatever, and they see Anglos that have been drinking, they don't know if there's going to be violence. They always have it in their heart that there just might be. (Montana, male)

This observation cuts to the core of the paramount theme that emerged over the course of the interviews: regardless of the region, or town, or tribal community, there was a very strong sense among the people interviewed that racial violence—hate crime—is endemic. That violence permeates the everyday lives of Native Americans is evident, in that most complained of multiple victimizations over the course of their lives. Rarely did they describe violent victimization as one-off affairs that touched them once and never again. There was always the sense, the fear, the expectation, that in the presence of nonnative Americans, they were vulnerable to harassment and attack. As one Minnesota man put it: "It's always there. I don't want to say it's a norm, but we get so used to it, we never know what's coming next, or where it's coming from. That's what it's like to be an Indian around here." This is typical of hate crime generally. While non-bias-motivated violence is a relatively infrequent occurrence for most people, bias-motivated incidents tend to be recurrent. Gay men and lesbians, Jews, immigrants, and other typical victims of hate crime come to anticipate the risk of victimization at every turn.

Ironically, so common is the violence and harassment that many claim to have ceased paying attention altogether. As one Native man said, "We get so used to it, some of us, most of us, just ignore it, let it wash away." And another: "You don't really notice it, it's so common. It's like an itch that's always there. After a while, it's just another irritation." Perhaps one of the most telling statements in this context comes from a Lame Deer resident who observed that he is "so used to it, when it's absent you don't know how to act. You are so used to the harassment and name-calling being around, you don't notice it until it is gone." He described for me his experiences in towns and cities away from the reservation, away from the state, where his reception was much warmer than in nearby border towns. He explained how he didn't feel the same animosity; how he was able to relax without fear of harassment. It was in those situations, he claimed, that he realized how bad things were on the reservation and in local communities. For this person and others like him, the discrimination, harassment, and violence had become so commonplace as to no longer be visible. Rather, it was so deeply ingrained in their life experiences that it has become part of the very fabric of their existence.

His story is especially revealing. It highlights how incessantly oppressive the reservation and border-town climate must be for so many Native Americans. So, too, does the following observation by a Wisconsin Native woman: "That racism is commonplace in the lives of the Native communities. It is almost like the sky. It is always there, right above everything that goes on, influencing your mood and your day, bearing down on you and inescapable." The experiences of the people in this community are not unlike the women in DeKeseredy et al.'s (2002) study of women in a Canadian public-housing development. Many of them also reported routine oppression, whereby they lived in constant fear of harassment or worse. While seemingly minor, the very pervasiveness of those petty actions—name-calling, being followed, etc.—is experienced as a violent form of oppression. Moreover, it is not readily apparent which of these acts might be a prelude to a more serious assault or battery.

It is also important, as I noted in chapter 3, to see harassment and violence through the prism of American Indians' social and individual histories. For them, any one incident of hate crime adds to the ledger of racism (Varma-Joshi, Baker, and Tanaka, 2004:191). As Varma-Joshi et al. describe it, indigenous peoples experience racist harassment and violence within the context of the history of colonization and segregation, and within the context of their own lifelong experiences of similar incidents. The combined personal and cultural biographies cultivate a sense of intergenerational grief and trauma that, according to Bubar and Jumper-Thurman (2004:74), "are the psychological fallout from federal policies that demeaned Native culture and used violence to force assimilation." It is this correspondence of the individual and the collective experience that both creates the problem and renders it normative. As an indelible part of their history, Native Americans come to *expect* harassment and violence whenever they come in contact with white people.

To those with whom we spoke, the violence seems unremarkable. Often, when asked if they perceived racial violence to be a problem in their communities, people interviewed would respond with an almost dismissive, "Oh yeah, of course." One Wisconsin man said, "Yeah, racial attacks are common in Indian Country, and of course Indian people have become calloused over the years, and when it happens, they don't think anything of it. It's just the way life is here." Consequently racial attacks are dismissed, rendered meaningless by their very pervasiveness. "The paradox," writes Scheper-Hughes (1996:889), "is that they are not invisible because they are secreted away and hidden from view, but quite the reverse." They are invisible because they are part of the fabric of daily life. To say that this is "everyday violence" is not to diminish its importance. Rather, it is to highlight the ubiquity and taken-for-grantedness of victimization:

> Anyway, I think race-motivated violence against Native Americans is common in the community, so I'm not sure it's unusual. There's a lot of Indian bashing. I just think that people get used to it, so they

don't say anything. I think I've, and all my friends and family and kids, we've all got lots of stories. You don't think about it, 'cause it's normal. You don't think about it until somebody like you comes, and you ask us. (Minnesota, female)

As this woman suggests, racial harassment and violence often go unnoticed because they are so common: they are unremarkable events when experienced in the context of daily collective and individual memories.

Another telling indicator of the constancy of racial violence and harassment was the sense of immutability expressed by so many members of the Native American community. There is a distressing fatalism in the general acceptance of the permanence of racism. That is, Native Americans expressed their belief that racism and its attendant forms of violence and harassment were so deeply embedded in their relationships with nonnatives that it would never cease to exist for them. Its presence had become commonplace and even "natural"; almost like the earth itself, racism was seen as an unchanging daily reality, regardless of what efforts might go into altering relationships:

It doesn't matter; we've tried this and that—cultural events, education, other get-togethers. And nothing changes. I'm still afraid, sometimes, to go some places. I still get harassed, and watched, and called names. It's never gonna be any different. That's just what being an Indian is like for us. (Utah, male)

It's bred in their genes. We were just born and they hate us. So you don't have to do anything to them really. There is nothing that I have to do to anyone, they are still gonna hate me, and they are still gonna hate Indians. You know, that's the way it is. (Minnesota, male)

Just as Feagin (2001:173) described the African American experience, being Indian in United States society "means always having to be prepared for anti-[Indian] actions by whites—in most places, at most times of the day, week, month, or year." Violence and the threat of violence appears to Native Americans in the communities I visited to be incessant and pervasive. It is not seen as unusual to be harassed in places of business, to be subject to racial epithets and name-calling on the street, to be pushed around in a bar, or to be beaten in the city park. As many said, that's the way it's always been and the way it will always be. Hate crime is unavoidable and impervious to change. Racial violence and the potential for racial violence are normal occurrences in Native American communities and reservation border towns. It has become an institutionalized mechanism for establishing boundaries, both social and physical. As a man from Montana described it, "Violence at any time is a pretty common thing, by Anglos, like saying that they're doing something that they think is inappropriate, like sitting in an alley or sitting on someone's car. It's a pretty narrow definition of what's appropriate or inappropriate, isn't it?" Hate crime thus plays a very real role in defining the acceptable range of roles and activities for Native Americans. It is one means by which to remind Native Americans where they belong, and do not belong.

It is also clear that there are social or political contexts in which Native American fears are most likely to be realized—in particular, times when those carefully crafted sociopolitical boundaries are challenged by Native people. As stated by one person, "You don't wanna stand up, like I always do, or you get trouble." So any efforts toward empowerment are commonly met with equally steadfast reactionary mobilizations. In particular, rights claims have triggered hostile and frequently violent reprisals from the anti-Indian movement (Rÿser, 1992; 1993; Grossman, 1999).

Reactionary Violence

A lingering and crucial element of the reactions of Native Americans to genocidal and ethnocidal practices by whites has been their continued demand for sovereignty and self-determination. Frequently this has been the invocation of specific rights claims—land, fishing, and resource rights. However it has been precisely these kinds of demands that have triggered anti-Indian violence (Rÿser, 1992; 1993; Grossman, 1999). This is perhaps not an unexpected development, since hegemony and the practices of insurgency are inherently dynamic and unstable. It is the case that "the insurgent process is one whereby subordinate group members introduce a particular tactic, the dominant group, over time, adjusts, counteracts, and often neutralizes that particular subordinate group strategy. . . . The end result of the struggle is often a reshaping of the existing stratification structure" (Roscigno, 1994:112). While I would argue that there is no ultimate end result of this ongoing process, Roscigno's point is well taken: counterhegemonic threats to the established racial order are consistently met with countermobilization on the part of the traditionally dominant group(s). In the context of colonialism, there is a long history of challenging its disempowering structures. Resistance on the part of the colonized has been as much a part of the dynamic of colonization as has been the violence of the colonizers. Here is, perhaps, where the links between colonial violence and contemporary patterns of hate crime are most clear. The reactionary violence that is described herein is a modern assertion of white privilege and dominance in the face of Native American efforts to maintain, if not redefine, their place as sovereign, rather than as dependent people.

When, on occasion, Indian people have challenged white privilege and asserted themselves through political activism, they have been victimized in order to silence their nonauthoritative claims. Efforts on the part of Native Americans to challenge the varied forms of oppression have elicited remarkably consistent patterns of such white reactionism. Native American nations and individuals who have resisted white encroachment have been exterminated, relocated, persecuted and prosecuted, harassed and beaten. The politics of recognition have been a dangerous game for Native Americans since the time of first contact. Nonetheless, struggles over identity, worth, and sovereignty continue throughout Indian Country, thereby threatening fundamental qualities of American Indian life and folkways. Traditional ways of living and interacting with the world are challenged legally, and just as frequently, extralegally, through violence.

This has been especially evident in the context of struggles over land and resources. In fact, Fixico (1998:189) would argue that the history of Native-nonnative conflict is predicated on divergent claims to the land and its resources, such that "in the history of Indian-white relations, the ownership of land has been greatly contested, with almost 2,000 wars and hostile engagements being waged. The outcome became one-sided by the late nineteenth century, and the legacy of exploitation continues today." Fixico's observations were reaffirmed in a number of interviews, as in the following:

> I think there's always been a sort of jealousy, too, about the land. It mostly comes down to the land. Our reservations are just a sliver of our former land holdings, but they want it all—still to this day, they want it all. We have to be forever vigilant about that. (Colorado, female)

Far from granting Indian nations' political sovereignty, the history of treaties with the United States federal government further diminished the identities, homelands, and freedom of the indigenous peoples. As Rÿser (1999, online) expresses it, "Indian land rights are paradoxically the strongest and weakest link in the mosaic of land rights in the United States." Too often, Native nations in the 1900s ceded great expanses of land in return for reserved rights to fishing, hunting, and other traditional ritual and subsistence activities, both on and off reservation lands. Despite such treaties, local and state officials from the 1960s to the 1980s consistently acted in ways that restricted those rights. In Washington, Oregon, and Wisconsin, to name three such states, game wardens and state legislatures conspired to abrogate resource treaties, thereby dramatically restricting Native access to fish and game (Institute for Natural Progress, 1992).

Native American activist Ramona Bennett aptly expresses the Native American response to this pattern of treaty abrogation when she writes that

> at this time, our people were fighting to preserve their last treaty right—the right to fish. We lost our land base. There was no game in the area . . . We're dependent not just economically but culturally on the right to fish. Fishing is part of our cultural forms and religion and diet, and the entire culture is based around it. And so when we talk about [Euroamerica's] ripping off the right to fish, we're talking about cultural genocide. (cited in Jaimes and Halsey, 1992:312)

Preexisting and ceded resource rights have been violently challenged through five hundred years of contact. Early European and Euroamerican assaults on Native American people revolved around conquests of land and minerals in particular. Contemporary assaults continue to revolve around the same resources, on a slightly different scale. In the name of preserving what few resources have been left to them, Native Americans since the 1960s have engaged in often dramatic politics of resistance. From the occupation of Pine Ridge, to the Northwest fish-ins, to litigation in Euroamerican courts, Native Americans have signaled their refusal to be deprived of their last treaty rights. Yet, as noted, these efforts toward empowerment are commonly met with equally steadfast reactionary mobilizations. Rights claims have triggered hostile and frequently violent reprisals from the anti-Indian movement (Rÿser, 1993). Writing of her experiences and observations in the Flathead Reservation in Montana, Kootenai Native Velda Friedlander-Shelby (1984, online) acknowledges this correlation: "As our Tribal Government becomes more active in exercising Tribal Sovereignty, the opposition heightens. Although it is not our intention to incite xenophobia on the part of whites living on the Reservation, such a condition has developed as we have increased the exercise of our rights to function as a sovereign Indian government." Similarly, the Wisconsin Advisory Committee to the U.S. Commission on Civil Rights (1989:2) concluded on the basis of public hearings that "racism against Indians had intensified as tribes have gained legal victories and have pursued educational and commercial developments."

The contemporary anti-Indian movement seeks to deprive Native Americans of the few rights ceded in exchange for massive tracts of land—on- and off-reservation fish and game rights, mineral resource rights, and water rights. For the most part, Native Americans have already lost their land base. Anti-Indian violence thus seeks to eliminate once and for all any claim American Indians have to what little remains by treaty and natural right. While few tribes have been spared the anti-Indian backlash, the effects have been especially evident in the Pacific Northwest, the Midwest, and among the Great Lakes Ojibwe. It is in these areas that the anti-Indian movement has been most organized and most violent in its efforts to thwart Native American assertions of treaty rights (Rÿser, 1993, 1999; Grossman, 1999; Pertusati, 1997).

Rÿser (1993) documents the emergence and spread of well-organized anti-Indian groups, including the Interstate Congress for Equal Rights and Responsibilities (ICERR); the Salmon-Steelhead Preservation Action for Washington Now (SPAWN); and Protect Americans' Rights and Resources (PARR). Collectively, these organizations fomented hostility toward Native Americans by claiming that tribal bodies were exploiting public sympathies and historical white guilt in an effort to gain access to natural resources, including water, land, and fish. Ostensibly premised on the notion of equal rights for all, the anti-Indian movement has denied the legitimacy of Native American rights claims. These groups have also engaged in quite tangible violations of Native American *human* rights, through ongoing harassment and violence against the tribal government and Native individuals (Grossman, 1999; Rÿser, 1992). The "fish wars" of the Pacific Northwest provide evidence of this, wherein the groups noted above led vividly confrontational demonstrations that frequently turned violent. Gunfire, rock throwing, and endangering Natives in their watercraft by creating wakes were some of the tactics used to frighten and intimidate Native spearfishermen. Vandalism of all kinds has been common: boats, nets, and parked cars have been targets of sabotage. All of this was embedded in a campaign of verbal taunts that employed the most hurtful and damaging racial epithets.

The current groundswell of resentment emerged initially as a response to the 1974 Boldt Decision (*United States v. Washington*). *Boldt* upheld tribal rights to salmon and spearhead fishing, granting the fourteen named tribes the rights to 50 percent of the salmon harvest. The resultant backlash was framed as a conflict of rights, wherein Native Americans were perceived to have been granted special rights, at the expense of the personal and property rights of nonnatives with land or other interests in Indian Country (Rÿser, 1992). Anti-Indian movement people acted on their beliefs in threatening and violent ways; Native American activists were specifically targeted. As one Native spearfishing activist put it,

> Those were really difficult days to live, you know? It wasn't easy, especially if you were doing as much as I was doing, all over the state of Wisconsin. I was a "bad Indian," the "most hated man in Wisconsin," because I wouldn't back down, hated for what I did to help my people preserve their rights. (Wisconsin, male)

Similar dynamics would become evident in the Great Lakes region in response to a related court decision. In 1983, the Voigt Decision (*Lac Courte Oreilles v. Lester B. Voigt*) affirmed the rights of the Chippewa in Wisconsin to hunt, fish, and gather on land ceded to the United States. Sport and commercial fishermen, threatened by the Ojibwe tradition of spearfishing, rallied in opposition throughout the 1980s and 1990s. Each spring, tribal declarations to invoke the right to spearfish received heavy media coverage. Unfortunately, there is little insight into how these declarations were carried out, or to the intensive efforts by tribes to balance tribal needs with those of other user groups. The public reaction to spearfishing thus included substantial hostility toward this little-understood—in fact, frequently misunderstood—tradition.

Following the *Voigt* decision, several antitreaty groups were organized in Wisconsin, including the Wisconsin Alliance for Rights and Resources (WARR); Equal Rights for Everyone (ERFE); Protect Americans' Rights and Resources (PARR); and Stop Treaty Abuse (STA). As with the antitreaty groups in the Northwest, these groups have used various methods to convince the public that the Ojibwe were out to "rape" the resources, overharvest deer and fish, and exercise their treaty rights without limitations—with the presumed result that they would destroy the entire tourist economy of Northern Wisconsin. In a PARR newsletter, one of its leaders opined,

> PARR has also been portrayed by some of you to be a racist organization . . . What some of you saw and reported as being racism was, in reality, something far different—it's protectionism, it's frustration, and it's a very deep concern about the future of tourism in Wisconsin, which is the same as saying a very real concern about ourselves and our ability to continue to earn a living in the North and in Wisconsin. (cited in Rÿser, 1992:33)

Reflections on this often willful misunderstanding of spearfishing were frequent in the interviews:

> Psychologically, it was like a kid playing with a toy. If he can't have that toy or do what you do, he's gonna be mad, there's gonna be animosity. This has really gotta be deeper. I have to blame their own people. No one gave them proper information, nobody took the initiative to pour water on the fire. In fact, they were fueling the fire. (Wisconsin, male)

Misunderstandings about the differences in the lives of many Ojibwe, and about Ojibwe hunting and fishing rights, led to strained Indian-white relations in Northern Wisconsin that intensified each time fishing season came around. Hunters and sports fishermen who opposed treaty rights confronted Indian fishermen at the lakes. Racial slurs and derogatory terms were shouted back and forth by both whites and Indians. The racism fueled by the spearfishing controversy became so intense that Indian and white children could not attend the same schools, nor could their parents eat at the same restaurants (Fixico, 1998). In 1988, spearfishing opponents went so far as to meet up with Native fishermen on the water, creating dangerous waves with their speedboats, coming just short of hitting their their boats, and constantly shouting racial epithets. Many of the people I interviewed had been involved in these conflicts, as in the following stories:

> I was out by the boat landing one night where there was over a thousand people chanting racial things. It got so they wouldn't allow our boats to come off the lake, so we had to take our trucks around, and boat trailers, to another landing . . . And I said, "Well, I'll take one, and another guy, too." We did our ceremonies and everything before

we left, and we did our water ceremonies when we were there. The stories that came out of that, especially the ones . . . how people would prepare themselves to be there at night. There was spearguns, there was pipe bombs, there was air guns, there was slingshots. One day we were setting the nets, and they were throwing rocks, and they were shooting, shooting wrist rockets, slingshots with ball bearings. One hit Sarah in her side and and knocked her to the bottom of the boat. I got hit, too. (Wisconsin, male)

We had people chase us, we had people follow us. We had threats, we had people pushing. When we would stand at the landings, they would come up behind us and they would push the backs of our knees, and they would throw lit cigarettes at us. They would spit on us, throw rocks. Death threats. My son—nuts were loosened on his tires on his van. He was coming home and he thought he had a flat tire, because his car started wobbling. So he stopped and all the lug nuts were loose. A lot of [tires], too, were slashed at the landings. (Wisconsin, female)

These are extreme cases of anti-Indian activity perpetrated against those who are most visibly engaged in challenging white norms of behavior for Native Americans. Yet retaliatory violence is not reserved only for those who take such vocal stands in the context of overt rights struggles. It awaits anyone who steps out of their appropriate place in the established hierarchy—those who are seen to be

climbing out of our buckskins, if you want to call it that, as Native peoples, and they don't like that. (Wisconsin, male)

Recall the Native American cited earlier who said, "Violence . . . is a pretty common thing, by Anglos, like saying that they're doing something that they think is inappropriate." Another Minnesota man cites a lengthy history of harassment in a number of contexts in which he apparently stepped out of line:

Yeah, you know, I don't know how much time you want to spend on this, I could go on for hours and hours about this stuff. When I was in Seattle, I had to get out of there because of the violence. I had to get out of White Earth because of the violence, you know. I'd been held hostage at gunpoint, and I had my car shot twice, I had my family threatened because of the positions I took, because of my activism.

Unfortunately, the posture of entitlement recently taken by Native Americans at the local, regional, and national level is often seen as an affront to white dominance, in that the activists are perceived to be violating the anticipated rules of behavior—that is, the rules of American apartheid. Instead of accepting their subordination, they resist it. In such a context, incidents of racial violence may escalate in retaliation. To paraphrase, the only good Indian is a quiet Indian:

> If you're an acceptable Indian—all right. If you're not, well that tends to work against you. There are good Indians and bad Indians. That's always there. So you can have advanced graduate degrees, but if you're a bad Indian, if you're visible or active, well . . . (Wisconsin, male)

Should they step outside the permissible boundaries that define a good Indian, they become vulnerable to retaliatory violence. Seen in this light, hate crime is a reactionary tool, a resource for the reassertion of whiteness over color. Racially motivated violence, then, becomes an extreme response to the Other who is out of control, who has overstepped his or her social or political or even geographical boundaries.

Ironically, retaliatory violence doesn't always have its intended effect. In the midwestern spearfishing conflict, the anti-Indian movement simply hardened the resolve of those determined to exercise their rights. So that rather than deter the spearfishing, anti-Indian activity drew more Chippewa back to their homeland, and back to their traditional lifeways. The significance of this will be made clearer in the concluding chapter.

Violent Police Encounters

Law enforcement agents are often the front line in efforts to keep the racialized Other within permissible boundaries. Indeed, police often play a leading role in legitimizing the use of violence against Native Americans and other minorities. There is a solid historical record of police engaging in violence intended to remind people of color of their subordinate status. Perhaps this is not surprising, in light of Williams and Murphy's (1998) observation that the modern United States police force emerged out of slave patrols. The legacy of this historical association is that police still carry out the role of keeping people of color in their place.

People of color may, at any time, cross the physical and social boundaries that otherwise insulate them from whites. This is where the police enter the picture; they are situated as guardians of these borders, charged to "protect whiteness against violence, where violence is the imminent action of that black [or red] male body" (Butler, 1993:18). Police violence is legitimate in this schema—considered a defensive act. Consequently, police violence is especially likely to occur where the victims have forgotten their place in the racial order.

This role has a lengthy history. Collective challenges to the authority of whiteness are as likely to elicit violence on the part of law enforcement agencies as on the part of any loosely organized anti-Indian movement. This has been especially apparent since the emergence of the civil rights challenges of the 1960s and 1970s: "As minority legal oppression became increasingly unbearable, particularly when minority members were literally denied control of their own communities, many rebelled. The ensuing racial protests, or as they were viewed by the dominant majority, 'riots,' and their suppression led to a shocking series of brutal, violent and lawless acts by law enforcement representatives throughout the country" (Mann, 1993:127).

The civil rights movement spearheaded by people of color initiated a series of challenges and reforms that tested the limits of the prevailing racial order. However, this profound insertion of difference into the currents of political and social life is not without resistance of its own. On the contrary, "strong opposition arose to confront the newfound assertiveness and proliferation of cultural difference that the movement had fostered" (Winant, 1997:30). While much of the opposition and corresponding violence sprang from the grass roots, state law-enforcement agents also played an integral role. Images of police dispersing crowds with fire hoses or tear gas are an indelible part of United States history. Missing and murdered civil rights workers—Native American, black, white, Jewish, and Latino—are also part of this legacy of resistance to civil rights advances.

At the forefront of state harassment and violence against minorities throughout the 1960s and 1970s was the FBI's Counter Intelligence Program—COINTELPRO. This institutional policy was initiated in 1941, largely to eliminate Communists. However, in the 1960s it was relaunched with the expanded mandate of disrupting and neutralizing dissident groups, specifically, Native American, African American, and Puerto Rican. In short, COINTELPRO was designed to prevent or eliminate the construction of collective oppositional racial identities.

As Ortiz (1981) reports, the American Indian Movement was a favorite target of police repression. Organized to resist the allocation and exploitation of Native American lands, and the more generalized oppression of Native peoples, AIM was fated to be seen as a dissident group that threatened the racial order. Nowhere did the campaign turn more deadly than on the Pine Ridge Reservation in South Dakota. AIM took a leading role in challenging a proposed transfer of mineral-rich land back to the federal government. In response, local police departments, the FBI, and a tribal ranger group—the GOONsquad—mustered massive resources and ammunition against the Native American organizers. In the end, dozens of Native Americans were killed, and hundreds more injured by gunfire, beatings, and being forced off the road while driving their cars (Messerschmidt, 1983). This modern-day "Indian war" took a tremendous toll:

> Even if only documented political deaths are counted, the yearly murder rate on the Pine Ridge Reservation between 1 March 1973 and 1 March 1976 was 170 per 100,000. By comparison, Detroit, the reputed "murder capital of the United States," had a rate of 20.2 per 100,000 in 1974. The United States average was 9.7 per 100,000. (Johnson and Maestas, 1979:83–84)

What these patterns of police brutality illustrate is that violence is considered an appropriate means with which to confront counterhegemonic racial mobilization. When blacks or Natives or Puerto Ricans organize to upset the racial balance, it is acceptable to forcibly put them back in their place. Those who cross the political, social, or cultural boundaries are legitimate victims of racial violence. So, too, are those who cross geographic boundaries. Those who do not belong are also subject to the coercive actions of law-enforcement agents, in a way that parallels the localized "move-in" violence perpetrated by other offenders. In both cases, victims are seen to have invaded areas where they do not belong.

Across North America, it has long been the case that aboriginal communities, like many other minority communities, are overpoliced. Again, this was borne out in the stories of those I interviewed. In the words of one,

> Law enforcement is more thorough with you. They ask more questions, spend more time. They just think you must have done something wrong. Even in a group of Indians and non-Indians, you will be grilled. A white guy will get a warning, an Indian will get interrogated

or even [be] charged with something minor. They're always looking for something to give you trouble for. (Montana, male)

This illustrates a key theme running throughout the interviews: that police appear to need little provocation to intervene against Native Americans, as opposed to the lack of intervention when they are victimized. For those interviewed, officers appear eager to explore perceived Native American wrongdoing, in contrast to nonnatives. For example:

When white people get killed everybody wants to know who, and to catch 'em, especially if they think it was an Indian. But not when an Indian gets *killed*. (Montana, female)

It is as if police are ready and willing to accept the mythology of the savage Indian, and act accordingly.

Racial profiling was broadly perceived by study participants to be a particularly widespread problem. Few such practices were seen to be as pervasive, or as effective, in putting Indians in their place and keeping them there. It demonstrates for its subjects—as if they did not know already—the spatial and cultural boundaries beyond which they must not travel. Racial profiling of Native Americans in and around reservations reinforces the historically conditioned patterns of segregation. This was disturbingly evident in the words of a Native man from Montana: "I've seen them just sit there by that bridge—that's the border—and they'll sit here all day and just keep stopping us when we have tribal plates. It's like, as soon as we leave the res, we're stopped for any or no reason. It makes you not wanna leave, you know?" This man's striking example underscores the sanctity of the reservation boundary. However, it is by no means an anomalous incident. From the perspective of many Native Americans, it appears to be a daily reality, especially in border communities where cultural boundaries are reinforced by geographical ones. Many reported their own experiences and observations of widespread police profiling of Native American drivers. This appeared to be especially the case where Native Americans were issued tribal license plates that clearly indicated their status. There was a widespread perception that this provided a powerful tool for singling out Native Americans and subsequently pulling them over with little or no reason. In the words of one woman from Minnesota, "There's a lot of harassing done by the police when they stop Indians with reservation plates." Once stopped, Native Americans are potentially subject to additional layers of disrespect, hostility, and occasionally, violence. An example at the lower extreme:

> Some people that I know come into town and leave town, usually they're stopped for something, and the cop really doesn't say for sure why they're stopping this driver. They've just been stopped, and there's no law that says, hey, this is the reason why I stopped you, but I found something else. There's a lot of that . . . And don't ever question them or ask why you were stopped. That really pisses 'em off, so they'll throw more charges at you. They just get mean and rude, call you names they shouldn't. (Montana, male)

Others told similar tales of police officers inventing charges, especially in the case of confrontational Native Americans. One Native woman described how a police officer invoked a litany of racial slurs in response to her challenging a speeding ticket, the amount of which was ultimately raised rather than lowered. It was, in fact, common for respondents to report the use of racist language when stopped by police.

Most significant, however, was the observation that upon stopping Native American drivers or pedestrians, police officers were not above using violence themselves. This appeared to be particularly the case for youth, who were most likely to share their own experiences of overly zealous stop-and-search practices. For example:

> We hate the cops 'cause they hate us. If they see a bunch of us together, they think the worst, they think we're in a gang or doing drugs or getting ready to do something wrong. They don't treat us right. Me, us—a lot of us—the cops give us a real hard time, like they're the boss. They'll stop us and ask us what we're doing, where we're going. They don't believe us, anyway. One time me and them two were going to play pool, but they stopped and gave us trouble, told us to get in the car. They started driving us around. Man, this is Farmington, that scared us. But they drove behind the school and made us get out, then started hitting us and kicking us. (New Mexico, male)

Like the assaults perpetrated by civilians described earlier in this chapter, police harassment and violence is also typically predicated on stereotypical images of Native Americans. The previous example shows the tendency of police to suspect the worst of a group of Native American youth seen together. To respond, as they did in this story, is to reinforce the tension that is inherent in the relationship between Native Americans and law enforcement. By acting on their biases, officers are recreating patterns that intensify the distrust that has long existed.

A woman from New Mexico told us about an incident she had observed at a local grocery store. Her example highlights the potential for violence when police carry negative images into their work. Here, the observer suspected that the standard drunken Indian stereotype was being used to justify mistreatment of a civilian:

> One time I went to Safeway, and there's this lady, she was standing in line over there, and the police, I guess somebody called, I don't know who called. She was standing around, bothering nobody, standing on the side of the phone booth, and here comes a cop. He stopped right there, and he grabbed the lady by the arm and pulled her over to the police car, and there was a little gap, I guess where the curb was right there, and somehow he pulled her over, we were just watching. I don't know how old she was, about forty to fifty, and she was kinda feeling good, minding her own business there, and here comes the police, grabs her, yanks her by the police [car], and I guess she didn't see the step down, maybe six inches, she almost fell. And the police grabs her back up and kind of twists her, and she was hurting, she was kind of crying, and he starts yelling at her. They figured, "drunk as a trunk, we don't care," and that's how they treated her. No respect for her, no trying to make sure she's not hurt.

In the cases just cited, police are thought to be responding to deeply ingrained stereotypes of Native Americans. However, they are as likely to react with hostility when Native Americans behave in unexpected, or inappropriate, ways. As noted earlier, challenges to the authority of police are especially likely to elicit a hostile, even violent, response, as in the following story:

> They would arrest you, and they won't just talk to you nice; they'll manhandle you, they'll kick you around. And I was coming down about two years ago, I saw a car, I could see the lights around the corner. I saw the flashing lights and I got out, and there were five squad cars, and . . . they had him sprawled out on top of the hood, sprawled out like that. It was dark, but I'd swear he was all bloody. So I pulled up and said, "Is there anything I can do here?" "Okay smart alec, keep on going." I kind of looked to see who he was. He said, "Did you hear what I said there, Red?" And he pushed me hard, out of the way, tried

to spin me around. And they were not nice. And that's the way they act down here, you know? (Minnesota, male)

For this man, such interactions with the police were a fact of life. He was a vocal community activist who says he often found himself at risk of being subjected to police violence. He says, "Every time I go to a demonstration, or when I've had a letter in the paper, or sometimes I go to court to help a friend—every time they conveniently pull me over, rough me up a bit, and then drive off." The clear message here: mind your place. A much more dramatic example from a Minnesota man active in the community shows the risk involved in confronting police:

My co-worker, or counterpart . . . he filed a lawsuit in the United States District Court, and it was going to be heard, it was on a Monday, you know, that's when it was scheduled to go to court. Well, that Saturday night, the same sheriff's deputy that was doing this stuff to these women out in Mayawash pulled him over, and he had been drinking some, but they pulled him over, impounded his car, took him home at, like, one thirty in the morning or something. And the next morning, when some other people stopped by, they walked into his house, and there he was, dead, and they looked at it and said, "Oh suicide." But the last person to see him alive was this sheriff's deputy, and you know, there was this court thing that was going to engage that following Monday. What finally ended up happening, my co-worker, my friend, he's dead, and that's how they left it, "Ah, he shot himself." The guy didn't own a gun, he was not a hunter, he was raised in the Twin Cities, but he wasn't raised on the reservation where all those skills evolved, he didn't own a gun, he wasn't a hunter type of a person, but . . . no investigation.

Ongoing, widespread brutality on the part of a single officer was at the heart of another story of police violence. A woman told the story of a policeman who had been coercing American Indian women to have sex with him, in this case, by threatening to frame the woman's boyfriend if she didn't comply. The sexual assaults on these women were perceived to be part of a broader pattern of disrespect and violence against the entire community. In addition to allegedly raping and sexually assaulting women, he was believed to have used excessive force in breaking up parties, especially those with high numbers of Native Americans in attendance. He was thought to be responsible for the destruction of personal property, as well as physical assaults on partygoers, kicking them and beating them with his nightstick.

Reports of police misconduct toward Native Americans, running the continuum from negligence to extreme forms of violence, were consistent across all the interviews, regardless of location. Like racial violence perpetrated by citizens, police mistreatment of American Indians appears embedded in the broader culture. Those interviewed described both under- and overenforcement in their communities. On the one hand, their own complaints were perceived to be trivialized or ignored; on the other hand, should they somehow draw attention to themselves—often simply by appearing in public—they ran the risk of becoming the target of police harassment and violence. As one Minnesota woman succinctly described the paradox,

> There's a lot of violence here, Indian on Indian, white on Indian, Indian on white. What makes it easy is the police are really bad. They don't do anything; worse, they beat Indians, especially young guys, real bad, and follow them, thinking they are always up to no good or in gangs. They'll go out of their way to pick up Indians. They just get treated different.

Jefferson (1994:254) has made a similar observation about the experiences of racial minorities in the United Kingdom, who have long seen police as "a hostile and alien force" that both aggressively enforces the law against blacks and Asians and turns a blind eye to racist attacks. As the participants in this study see it, the same patterns hold for them: they can neither trust the police to respect their rights, nor to protect them when others violate their rights.

Considering their experiences, it should come as no surprise that American Indians fail to report victimization to the police. Police are the most immediate, visible symbol of what is perceived to be a racist state. Consequently, they are not the authorities to whom Native Americans turn for help. The legacy of distrust runs too deep. This lack of trust is not misplaced. One Wisconsin man highlighted the frustration that inhibits reporting victimization to the police, stating that "victims see little use in registering complaints with an unsympathetic white justice system, or even with tribal law enforcement authorities." Some people pointed to an enabling climate, in which racial violence is allowed to flourish. This view was expressed by a man from Montana who observed that "there's a lot of incidents that never get reported—who ya gonna file a complaint with? The county? The state? The feds? Nobody trusts them, they're a big part of the problem." Ironically, the comments of the white police officers who were also interviewed lend credibility to the observations of these tribal members. One officer stated quite frankly that "much of the distrust between communities is the fault of the Native people, who think everyone is racist and is discriminating. The tribe brings stereotypes upon themselves, and use stereotypes. They use the notion of the white man as a political ploy to get tribal votes." Another officer, whose comments bear repeating, was a little more subtle, though no less racist in what he had to say. In spite of the extent of violence and harassment revealed in the interviews, this officer claimed that violence was not widespread, and that

> The majority of people just want to get along. Go about their business, live their lives, don't want any problems and they won't do anything of a prejudiced nature, that wouldn't be considered a hate crime because they wouldn't want to get involved in something like that. They're overall just good law-abiding citizens, there are just a few bad apples that love to instigate a little problem and looking for a scapegoat in life and it is always easy to blame one race no matter which race it is. Blaming another for some type of problem (Wisconsin, male).

With such willful blindness, it is no wonder that tribal members have little faith in local law enforcement. And where police fail to intervene, they give permission to hate, implying as they do that Native Americans are not worthy of protection (Perry, 2001). As I have argued elsewhere, discriminatory practices by the state and by state actors send a powerful message about the worth, or lack thereof, of its targets. Political discourse and action reaffirms and legitimates the negative evaluations of difference, which gives rise to hate crime. Thus I accept van Dijk's (1995:2) thesis that discourse is central to the "enactment, expression, legitimation and acquisition" of bigotry of all types, including hate-motivated violence. The state is a contested site, wherein the "deliberate use of hate by rhetors is an overt attempt to dominate the opposition by rhetorical—if not physical—force" (Whillock, 1995:xiii). Law enforcement agents enact the power of law and its identity-making capacities through their actions on Others. State personnel construct identity through ongoing practices that institutionalize specific and normative forms of race. In particular, they engage in "derivative deviance," or violence perpetrated on the marked Others, who are "presumed unable to avail themselves of civil protection" (Harry, cited in Berrill and Herek, 1992:290). In other words, the state itself acts as a victimizer, thereby validating the persecution of gender and racial minorities.

The perception that police are not interested in intervening in cases of anti-Indian activity, along with the perceived frequency of victimization, leave Native Americans feeling vulnerable to ongoing racial harassment and violence. Combine this with the overwhelming stereotyping and oppression that contextualizes and facilitates such violence, and hate crime frequently has the intended effect of maintaining the marginal, often demonized, status of American Indians. As the next chapter will show, the cumulative impacts of the cultural and social histories of victimization do indeed wear its victims down.

7

The Cumulative Effects of Hate Crime

In the previous chapter, I noted that what many Native Americans experienced was an ongoing *process* of victimization. That is, rarely did their victimization involve a single incident. Rather, it was a recurring pattern for them. As Bowling (1998:230) expresses it, "Victimization and racialization—the processes by which a person becomes a victim of this form of crime—are cumulative, comprised of various encounters with racism, some of which may be physically violent, some lying only at the fringes of what most people would define as violent or aggressive." Not surprisingly, then, the toll that anti-Indian activity takes is also cumulative in its effects. Any single event may appear relatively benign when seen on its own. Yet when direct and indirect victimization are experienced as ongoing and pervasive, the impact can be very dramatic for its subjects. Recall the previous argument that racist violence is interpreted by its victims in the context of both personal and cultural biographies of colonization and violence. Each discrete incident is lived as part of an historical pattern of victimization. Cumulatively, they can have the intended effect of overwhelming their targets.

This is something that has been largely missed in the hate-crime literature. The focus has mostly been on the immediate physical (e.g., Levin and McDevitt, 1993) and psychological impacts of hate crime on its victims (e.g., Herek, Cogan, and Gillis, 2002; McDevitt et al., 2001). However, most of this work fails to look at the cumulative, long-term impact of hate crime on victims and their communities. As noted above, the victimization described in my interviews was systemic; it was not a single event. Rather, violence and the threat of violence were constants for the Native Americans interviewed. It is this normativity that engenders especially dramatic reactions. Trask (2004:13) suggests the continuum on which these responses might lie: "Colonized people, like colonized cultures, are no longer open, dynamic, and fertile. Once colonized, they become moribund, oppressed, segregated, closed, or apathetic." Indeed, there is some evidence of each of these in the reactions of people to whom we spoke.

"You Just Get Tired": Oppression through Violence

Those whom I have interviewed describe an array of individual and collective reactions, many of which were indicative of the aggregate impact of normative, systemic victimization. One man from Montana stated the impact very simply: "A lot of it is petty stuff. But it's the petty stuff that gets to you after a while, because it's all the time." The descriptions of the impact remind one of a form of water torture, wherein the constant *drip, drip, drip* on the forehead ultimately unhinges its subject. Consider, too, Marilyn Frye's (2004) analogy of the birdcage. If one were to look only at one wire of the cage, it would be difficult to understand why the bird does not escape. Yet when taken as a whole, it is clear that the bird is constrained by a network of wires. Similarly, the regular barrage of otherwise mundane and seemingly trivial forms of harassment ultimately disempowers the victims of racial violence. Shoving, spitting, taunts of "timber nigger" and "go back to the res" are the metaphorical equivalent of the *drip, drip, drip,* or the wires of the cage. These incessant, pervasive microaggressions, along with more serious forms of victimization, wear down their victims, as intended. It is the collective impact of multiple incidents that renders hate crime so debilitating. This corresponds to Feagin's (2001:196) observation that "for any given individual, repeated encounters with white animosity and mistreatment accumulate across many institutional arenas and over long periods of time. The steady acid rain of racist encounters with whites can significantly affect not only one's psychological and physical health but also one's general outlook and perspective." Among my Native American study participants, there were many whose stories supported Feagin's contention, especially concerning outlook and perspective. Indeed, there was a generalized sense of feeling weighed down, oppressed by the ongoing threat of harassment and other racist actions:

> You just get tired. You don't want to have to face it anymore. After a while, you hate to go into town, 'cause ya know as soon as you cross that line, somebody's gonna do something—yell at ya, curse ya, maybe chase you back across the river. Sometimes it's just too much. (New Mexico, female)

> It wears us down, ya know? We don't have to do anything. We're just there, and someone calls us a "lazy Indian," or an "Indian whore," and maybe they throw stuff, or one time someone spit on me—I didn't do

anything! It's that stuff every day or every week that gets to me. I just don't wanna have to face any white people. (Colorado, female)

The perception of recurrent threats and harassment leaves its victims feeling disempowered. It is, as many expressed, "overwhelming," "tiring," "wearing." Confronting the reality and potential of racialized victimization can drain the energies of those subject to it. The cumulative individual and collective histories of systemic violence take a dramatic toll on its victims. A growing body of literature, for example, points to the elevated rates of long-term emotional and psychological harm suffered by hate-crime victims (e.g., Herek, Cogan, and Gillis, 2002; Iganski, 2003; McDevitt et al., 2001).

As I will discuss further in the following section of this chapter, the consequences of this persistent pattern of threat are manifest in an array of related behavioral practices, including withdrawal and isolation. This is, of course, the goal of hate crime perpetrators: to force their victims to give up, to return to the reservation, for example. And indeed, this is an all-too-common response on the part of actual and vicarious victims alike.

Staying Put: The Segregating Effect of Hate Crime

For too many American Indians, the perception, if not the reality, of "what's out there," that is, outside of the reservation, has its intended effect of keeping people in their place. It reinforces the social and geographical boundaries that Native Americans are not meant to cross. It contributes to ongoing withdrawal and isolation. In short, it furthers historical patterns of segregation. Through violence, the threat of violence, or even through the malevolent gaze, Native Americans are daily reminded that there are places where they are not welcome:

There were places you just didn't want to go. Like Mercer and all— that's where the head of the Ku Klux Klan lives. That's only fourteen miles from here. There's just places you don't wanna go, you don't feel safe. Really, you don't feel safe when you go off the res. (Wisconsin, female)

There is just places where you get in, you know, you are not supposed to be in there. I guess there is, there's a kind of sense, places—for

Indians and non-Indians in the communities around here—there is an idea that Indians have a certain place; that there is a certain way that they are supposed to behave when they are on the communities. And like in the South compared to this area is the Deep North, you know. The whole sense of maintaining one's place and one's position in society is the kind of feeling that Indian people get around here. (Wisconsin, female)

For some, the constancy of the fear is almost paralytic. At the very least, it limits their desire to interact with white people. For others, it limits their movements and their perceived options, resulting in withdrawal. It creates "more borders," said one Wisconsin woman, in that people become fearful of moving out of the relative safety of the reservation. They "stay here for all their lives, because they're afraid to go out there because of what's going on, for all of these reasons." Very similar sentiments were expressed by others:

Oh man, it's like all the time. You don't wanna go anywhere they are—I'm afraid a lot when I come to town. I always think someone is going to beat me up, 'cause every weekend something bad happens. I've been followed and beat up a couple of times, people throw things at you, spit at you on the street. They say all the things you hear—call me a squaw, tell me I'm stupid, tell me I don't belong. I'm from the res, and they know that, and they tell me to stay away from their town. (Wisconsin, female)

These violent reminders contribute to ongoing withdrawal and isolation, thus furthering historical patterns of segregation. The hostility and violence experienced "out there" produces what Wachtel (1999:221) characterizes as "voluntary segregation," wherein those subject to the discriminatory and hateful patterns of behavior may choose to return or simply remain in the relative safety of the reservation. In some respects, little has changed since the nineteenth century:

It's at that point, 1884, that then the Crows are told that they can't cross the reservation boundaries any longer, they have to stay within the reservation boundaries, and there's actually a word, I can't think of the word for it, but there's a word for living within the line, that's what they were told, that there's a line on the ground, living within the line on the ground is what it means. They were told that they couldn't cross that line on the ground even though they couldn't see it. But, correlated to that is that non-Indians, then, especially with that sort of pioneering attitude, took on this sort of vigilantism that if Crows did cross the line, that they had the right to kill them, or at least hurt them. (Montana, male)

Nonnatives tend to think of reservations only as places of poverty and despair. This is only a part of the story, for they are also home for many people. They are akin to bell hook's notion of the "home place," which represents a safe place where black people can gather and express themselves *as* themselves (hooks, 1990:42). Reservations—with all of their faults—also represent safety, identity, heritage. They "act like forcefields, pulling Indians together" (Valaskakis, 2005:245). But Wachtel (1999:221) warns us not to mistake this as a free choice. Rather, choosing to live in an isolated enclave "as a 'preference' over living with people who don't want to live with you is not equivalent to simply preferring to be separated."

It is clear from the work of Massey and Denton (1993) and Wachtel (1999) that the effects of residential segregation, like that encapsulated in the reservation system, has dramatic implications for other forms of marginalization. Isolation on the reservation frequently (re)creates the related patterns of social and economic segregation noted in chapter 5. There are what Wachtel (1999:219) refers to as "reciprocal relationships" between housing segregation and other forms, such as health, education, and employment. Residential segregation creates barriers to an array of related amenities, such as high-quality schools and public services, or affordable housing. Thus the tendency to physically marginalize indigenous peoples, the attempts to keep them on the reservation, finds its parallel in the tendency to also socially marginalize them. Indians and non-Indians thus live a life apart in and around reservations. Again, in light of the potential for exclusionary violence, this is not a voluntary choice but rather the safe choice. Rather than risk the threat of being forcibly removed from public places, many Native Americans opt to retreat to their own stores, bars, restaurants, or other gathering places.

Residential segregation ensures economic isolation as well. This is especially significant for rural reservations, since "Indians in rural areas are subject to the risk of being dependent upon fewer economic sectors, and rural reservation businesses face the disadvantage of smaller consumer markets. Moreover, access to urban markets plays a critical role in determining the financial and employment success of Indian ventures"

(Taylor and Kalt, 2005:4). On reservations, this is especially clear in the elevated rates of unemployment and poverty. Native Americans are among the most impoverished, with 32 percent of reservation Indian families living below the poverty line in 2000, and more than 20 percent living in deep poverty. (For a family of four, the federal poverty rate is $16,895; "deep poverty" refers to those with a household income that is less than 75 percent of the poverty rate.) They also experience elevated rates of unemployment. Nationally the average rate of unemployment for Native Americans living on reservations is about 20 percent (and even higher on some reservations), much higher than the 6 percent national average (Taylor and Kalt, 2005). The impact of this economic marginalization is evident in dramatically heightened rates of alcoholism, malnutrition, infant mortality, suicide, and early death by accident and disease (Bachman, 1992; Beauvais, 1996; Jaimes, 1992a).

The job options on most American Indian reservations are limited in number, and certainly limited in terms of income. These diverse forms of segregation, like residential segregation, are also reinforced through racially motivated violence. Even when Native Americans step beyond the reservation boundaries to take a job, or as we suggested earlier, to go to school, they may be left vulnerable to harassment and violence as a reminder that they have transgressed social as well as geographical boundaries:

> That's why people don't leave, why they don't go into the towns to look for a job. They're afraid to go there, so they stay inside. They know—from their experience, or their family's, or their friends—what can happen. There's too much risk out there. (Arizona, female)

Racist threats may await Native Americans when they seek employment off the reservation. This is not an atypical experience for racial minorities. Workplace violence directed against racial and ethnic minority employees is relatively common. In fact, the presumption of racial hierarchies has had, and continues to have, a profound impact on the place of minority groups within the labor process. In particular, people of color have traditionally been marginalized and exploited as free, cheap, and malleable labor (Young, 1990). Thus while the political and social gains made by minorities in recent years threaten white cultural identity, economic gains represent a more direct and tangible threat to white economic security. People of color who presume to advance on the economic ladder are perceived as unfair and undeserving competitors, and takers of white jobs. People of color are seen to have overstepped the economic boundaries that have long contributed to their marginalization. Consequently, in the context of economics, white fear and resentment are commonly and viciously translated into racial violence.

Where once whiteness guaranteed status and security, this is no longer the case. Gone are the days when minorities could legitimately be excluded from rewarding job opportunities. Gone, too, are the days of plentiful industrial and manufacturing jobs that offered white males the resources for constructing dominant racial and gender identities: family wage and physical labor. The massive economic restructuring that has taken place in the United States over the last two decades has resulted in a shift from industrial to service jobs—the latter providing significantly less opportunity for constructing an aggressive and masterful white masculinity.

Many white men now picture and present themselves as the new minority. They experience a sense of displacement and dispossession relative to people of color. This imagery of white-man-as-victim gives voice to the insecurity of white men in a weakened economy. It also provides an ideological rationale for recreating people of color as legitimate targets for retaliatory violence. This has become evident in the studies of workplace ethnoviolence carried out by the Prejudice Institute (Weiss, Ehrlich, and Larcom; 1991–1992; Ehrlich, 1998), which find relatively high rates of harassment and defamation of people of color, that is, those who don't belong. Successive reports of the United States Commission on Civil Rights (1990; 1992a; 1992b; n.d.) also reveal the links between hostility toward affirmative action, and violence against minorities.

Fearing a loss of domestic and global hegemony, white perpetrators of racially motivated violence seek to redeem their status through repressive and retaliatory acts of violence. They seek to enhance their own stature and mastery by simultaneously vanquishing the Other, who has overstepped geographical and economic boundaries. While examples of workplace violence were relatively rare among participants in my study, they did occur, as the following examples attest.

My kids, they have enough trouble at school. Then they tried to do summer jobs, and they don't wanna do that no more. They worked up at the ice cream place there, and white guys would talk mean to them. My girl was afraid 'cause of what they said, that they were gonna get her. Kept saying things like when did she get off work, they'd be back then, and did she taste good as the ice cream? Nobody told them to go away. Her boss just laughed. I told her she didn't have to go back. (Colorado, female)

I don't wanna work there. I tried but didn't like it. Nobody wanted me there. Things they said, called me, you know, "chief," "Injun Joe." And then they always played jokes, like put posters on the wall with dead Indians 'n stuff. They scared me 'cause I thought that was me, they were gonna get me. I had a couple notes left on the counter, said things about dead Indians, how they were quiet. I can take a hint. So I left there a couple weeks later. (Minnesota, male)

Many other American Indians also "take a hint" and migrate between jobs, or even back to the reservation, to escape violence or the threat of violence. As with housing segregation, they return to their own people rather than risk the hostility of white America. Workplace violence perpetuates the patterns of job segregation, wherein Native Americans are relegated to low-skill, low-wage positions, or alternatively, no work at all.

In an effort to enhance job opportunities, many American Indians have taken the chance of moving on to postsecondary education. Their involvement in higher education over the last four decades has been both encouraging and disheartening. Throughout the 1980s and 1990s, admission rates improved, but only marginally (Pavel, 1999). Much of the increase has been attributed to federal educational initiatives, one of which was to significantly enhance funding for tribal students. The second important movement was toward self-determination in American Indian education, resulting in the establishment of tribally controlled colleges, of which there are now twenty-four, serving more than ten thousand students (Wright, 1991; Mihesuah, 1996).

The persistent underrepresentation of Native Americans in higher education is accounted for in part by their high rates of attrition: a substantial number fail to return even after the first year of study (Wright and Tierney, 1991; Wright, 1991). These high dropout rates have been attributed to a constellation of factors, including lack of academic preparation, loneliness and family problems, lack of support, and lack of role models (McIntosh, 1987). Together these factors create an alien, often hostile environment for Native American students. At the extreme, "Native American students face cultural insensitivity and sometimes prejudice by administrators, service workers, faculty and non-Indian students" (Juan, cited in Wright, 1991:7). Add to that the risk of violence, and schools and universities are not exactly desirable places to spend any length of time. This was apparent from the experiences of both high school and university students who participated in my studies.

A campus hate-crime survey of Native American students yielded disturbing findings as well (Perry, 2002). In all, thirty-six (40 percent) of those students responding reported that they had been victimized by virtue of their race, for a total of approximately 130 incidents. This is somewhat higher than the national trends suggested by Ehrlich (1998; 1999). Moreover, twenty-eight of those victimized indicated that they had been victimized multiple times. For the most part, these victimizations involved some form of verbal insult or harassment (23.9 percent and 15.2 percent, respectively). Only two respondents had themselves experienced physical threats, and none reported that they had been physically attacked. Eight students reported some other form of ethnoviolence, such as being ignored or mistreated by campus staff. Among the incidents described by students was the following typical example:

> As me and my friends were walking back from the clubs to the vehicle, a group of guys walked up behind us and told us to go back to the res, and told us, chiefs don't need to belong here. Me and my friend were walking to Target, midday, and a vehicle of boys drove by and threw some empty bottles at us and told us the same thing, and that we shouldn't be here. (Arizona, male)

A female student at a Minnesota university shared a similarly disheartening story:

> Well, people don't want you here, they stare at you. They call you names—at a university! Ya think it's okay here, but it's not really. I had one girl come up and spit in my face and say, "I hate dirty fucking Indians. You should go back to the reservation." She spit, and I'm dirty? I would rather not be in that place, so I go where I'm safe, I go to Indian Studies. You know, it's just, you know, feeling welcome, like you're [inaudible] like here you go, you know if someone you know is going to be walking through that door any time, and you can sit and talk, where in Memorial, you know, they'll be like a hundred students coming in before you recognize one friend coming in. Here it's just better, here you can see more people that you know.

As these examples reveal, students perceive themselves to be frequent victims of racial bias and harassment. Their experiences suggest that even the university can be a hostile environment for Native American students. It is a disturbing paradox that, as a 1989 commission on racism concluded, "Racism against Indians had intensified as tribes have gained legal victories and have pursued educational and commercial developments" (Wisconsin Advisory Committee to the U.S. Commission on Civil Rights, 1989:2). And on college campuses, as on the streets of reservation border towns and in the workplace, this racism can and does take the tangible form of racially motivated hate crime.

Getting Back: Antiwhite Sentiment and Violence

I was at the boat landings. That was, what? fifteen years ago, and I'm still haunted by that violence, that hatred. I still can't believe how angry and cruel they were. I was never seriously hurt—pushed around, spit at, had rocks thrown, a lot of threats. But it still really scared me, 'cause I knew any minute it could get worse. So I'm still afraid, I still don't trust a lot of white people. Some people I thought were friends were on the other side. You don't forget that, you stay hurt and angry. So I don't want much to do with them. I don't like them any more than they like me. (Wisconsin, female)

Another area that remains largely unexplored in the broader hate-crime literature is the impact of victimization on the victim's perceptions of the offender and his or her group. If we are to understand the collective and cumulative effects of ethnoviolence on broader intergroup relationships, it is important to first understand how victimization—even the act of offending—affects the perceptions of the people directly involved in the offense. This is something about which we have little, if any, information. The statement that opens this section begins to give us some hints.

Scant attention has been paid to the notion that anxiety triggered by the victimization of one's cultural group can easily erupt into periods of retaliatory violence. In the U.S., Chief Justice Rehnquist acknowledged this, writing for the majority in *Wisconsin v. Mitchell* (1993). He argued for the recognition of hate crime as a special class of offense because of the likelihood that it would, in fact, initiate yet more violence. This effect was evident in New York following the murder of a young African American man by a crowd of Italian youth in Bensonhurst in

1989, where the murder was followed by days of racial skirmishes. A more recent example occurred in Carson City, Nevada, in 2002, where a group of twelve American Indian males attacked two Latino males, apparently in response to an earlier assault on a Native American in which they were thought to have taken part. McDevitt et al. (2001) include a retaliatory motive in their typology of hate-crime offenders, based on their observation that a notable proportion of offenders reported that their offense was a response to a prior (perceived or real) offense perpetrated against them. But again, the efforts to establish this link are few, and tend to rely on anecdotal evidence. The observations of the Native Americans featured in this study provide some cumulative evidence to support this supposition. Especially for the youth interviewed in this study, the legacy of indifference, hostility, and brutality toward minority communities "breeds consequences. When any minority group experiences injustice at the hands of the dominant society, anger, frustration and agony are bred" (Boldt, 1993:60). So, too, are the roots of resistance sown. Native American youth, consistently treated to disrespect, harassment, and violence, respond to their brutalization with attempts to gain both racial and gender recognition through challenging or confrontational behavior. On the one hand, such behavior serves notice that the person in question does not accept his or her subordination. On the other hand, for young males especially, it is a peer display of one's toughness, fearlessness, and solidarity.

> What I'm seeing in the school system is the discipline problems. From fourth grade up. Then once they get into high school, they won't drop, but from fourth grade to eighth, there's a lot of violence, the ones where they have cops patrolling the halls. And they're starting to get a little angry, the kids are, 'cause they are tired of the white kids harassing them all the time. They get kicked around, shoved down and into the walls and stuff. And some of them have about had it. I think there are going to be more fights, 'cause the Indian kids aren't going to take it anymore. They want to get back now. Now you'll see the police and the guys in the office pay attention—when it's white kids getting hit. They don't care when it's us, but don't let *them* get hurt. No wonder the kids are pissed. (Montana, female)

Thus another damaging cumulative effect of the daily threat of harassment is that it cultivates antiwhite sentiment, and ultimately, antiwhite violence. Even if the victim's cultural group does not directly retaliate against the hate-crime perpetrators or their reference community, hate crime may nonetheless have deleterious effects on the relationships between communities. Cultural groups that are already distant by virtue of language differences, or differences in values or beliefs, are rendered even more distant by the fear and distrust engendered by bias-motivated violence. Intergroup violence and harassment further inhibits positive intergroup interaction. For instance, several Native Americans interviewed spoke of the way their harassment exacerbates anger toward, and distrust of, whites.

> I just get so mad sometimes. Why do they have to do that? Why do they follow me and call me names? Or try to scare me? It makes it so I don't want to have nothin' to do with them. Why would I? They hate me, so I kinda feel the same way. (Colorado, male)

For some, anger spills over into action. Some reported hearing of, witnessing, or engaging in retaliatory violence against whites. Again, it was the daily barrage of insults, slights, harassment, and surveillance that engendered bitterness that some were consequently unable to contain: "For many of the Native people, we hit a boiling point of pent-up frustrations and anger at the racism and ignorance, and the fact that we feel powerless to fight, and we explode." One educator described her perception of retaliatory violence in the schools:

> It goes both ways. The Indian kids come here, maybe from the reservation schools, or at least from the reservation. And they're already angry when they get here, so it doesn't take much for them to react when someone calls them "chief," or tells them to go back to the reservation, or bumps into them, intentionally or not, in the hall. These kids live with it everyday, and at some point, some of them turn around and give some back. (Wisconsin, male)

Another participant related his biography:

> I grew up on the reservation, and as a kid, and now, it was always the same. I didn't trust white people because I felt like they were always hassling me and my friends and family—everybody. Or they were ignoring us. Either way, we were treated racist. Sometimes I ignore it, but sometimes I fight back. I call names, I've even hit people who crossed the line, especially when they hollered at my wife or something. I'm not proud of it, but dammit, I do have to get even sometimes. (Montana, male)

And yet another man speaks to the cyclical nature of anti-Indian/anti-white violence, and what he sees as likely consequences:

> Out there, it's hatred against Native Americans. The Cheyenne, we're prejudiced against whites because of distrust, not hatred . . . And when we act against the constant slurs, we sometimes react with violence, and then we go to jail. That doesn't happen to the whites. (Montana, male)

The last observation is especially illuminating. The speaker attests to the reality, and basis, of antiwhite retaliatory violence. But he also alludes to one unfortunate consequence of such retaliation—it inadvertently reinforces white perceptions of Native American criminality. Rather than treat such violence as part of a provocative cycle, white culture and often the white criminal-justice system reacts in a way that must further embitter Native Americans. The cycle of distrust begins anew. And the anger intensifies.

Turning the Violence Inward: Internalized Racism and Intraracial Violence

"Shame, shame and self-contempt!" (Fanon, 2000:260)

In contrast to those who turn their anger outward toward their victimizers are those who have internalized the bitterness and resentment. Paolo Freire (1970:31) refers to this as internalized oppression, by which he means "the oppressed having internalized the image of the oppressors and adopted his guidelines." What emerges for those who have adopted this stance is antagonism and hostility directed toward oneself and one's community. Their rage at their continued disempowerment is misdirected inward or downward or sideways, toward those who are similarly victimized, rather than upward toward those who are responsible for their oppression. McClain and Stewart (1995:149) fall just short when they assert that "we must remember that racial minorities, having been socialized in a society that sees them as inferior to whites, are equally likely to believe in the inferiority of racial groups other than their own." It is important to interpret such anxiety within the master narrative of white, heterosexual, masculine hegemony. That is, intraracial hostility, even violence, is not about intraracial conflict per se. Rather, it is about how these tensions play out in the context of relations of racial-ethnic-gender subordination. Ultimately, hegemonic constructions of race or gender identity infuse the experiences and interactions within subordinate groups as well. It is not only groups other than their own that are perceived as inferior but also the group that *is* their own:

> But I think powerlessness brings you to the point where there's violence, and hate that comes through, and it gets so difficult to separate it out. That's why I think it's important to talk about hate and call it what it is, whether it's discrimination, whether it's prejudicial. 'Cause in the end it makes us hate ourselves, too. (Minnesota, female)

Racism—and the racist violence that is featured here—shapes all audiences. Both the oppressor and the oppressed fall prey to its seductiveness. Five hundred years of contempt, degradation, and violence cannot help but fill the minds of Native Americans with the discourses that Euroamericans have used to marginalize and subdue them. The imagery of which I wrote in chapter 4, reinforced by hate violence, has taken root in the psyches of many Native Americans, such that they develop a parallel loathing for themselves and their race. So pervasive are the constructs that present Native Americans as inferior Others that the power of such concepts becomes irresistible for some. The Western image of American Indians becomes mirrored in their self-definitions and to other American Indians. They adopt a "colonized mentality" (Padilla, 2001). Poupart makes this argument explicitly in an attempt to comprehend rising rates of familial and intimate violence in Native American communities. As American Indians, she asserts, "we internalize meanings of difference and abject Otherness, viewing ourselves with and through the constructs that defined us as racially and culturally subhuman, deficient, and vile" (Poupart, 2003:87). A Native American man from Minnesota speaks firsthand about the reality of this theoretical construct:

> It's like a self-fulfilling prophecy, you know? As you grow up, society tells you that you're second class, and you wake up and you look in the mirror and you don't like what you see. Then anybody is also a mirror image—you're not going to like them, either. If you don't love yourself, you sure as hell ain't going to give a shit about anybody else who's Native, and you see that in black communities also. You know, you think how can people treat each other that way? How can they be so cold and unfeeling and cruel?

Internalized racism is thus an historical artifact of colonization. Earlier I stressed the need to consider the experience of hate crime within *both* the individual and cultural histories of its victims. This aids in understanding the contemporary manifestations of internalized racism. "American Indians' knowledge of our historical and continuing oppression is experienced as a profound anguish" (Poupart, 2003:88), a "soul wound" to the spirit of Native American people that is evident in a cumulative rage that often has no safe outlet (Duran and Duran, 1995). The safe alternative, then, is to deflect the pain inward, toward the self or other American Indians (Padilla, 2001; Poupart, 2003). The historicity of the process is recognized by one Minnesota Native man who was himself a victim of it:

> Yeah, and I think that's another factor, but I think if you work, the whole equation [goes] back to, "How did we get here?" "Why are you and I having this conversation?" Pick a starting point—say, two hundred years ago—let's look at everything that's happened to this indigenous community in those two hundred years, you know? Look at the hundreds and thousands of Indian children who had a situation similar to mine in public schools, look at the effects of multiple generations of this structural racism, this structural white supremacy, and you see one hell of a lot of kids these days who grew up in Bemidji High School, and a hell of a bunch of kids fought Indian kids. And I'm not even sure why, but they're hostile, they're angry, they're upset, they're right on the edge, they could go either way on you, you know, in a moment's notice. And that sense of hopelessness and despair that comes with, "You're a no-good, dirty, stupid, stinking Indian"—the family that that child came from, the parents, "no-good, dirty, stinking, stupid Indian"—the grandparents of that child, same thing—and you can go on back to great-grand.

A Wisconsin man indicates how his familial and personal biography coincided with, and was shaped by, historical practices of deculturation:

> There were some Indian Studies classes and some Ojibwe language classes that I wanted, and that Ojibwe language was a three-year sequence, 'cause I wasn't raised with my language, because my parents were of that generation where [it was] just really taken out of them in a mean and hostile way. I mean the things that they did to my mother were horrible. So there's a lot of them out there who

really don't want anything to do with being an Indian, because being an Indian meant so much pain and hurt and anger and confusion, and all that. So they assimilated to the extent that they could, which meant I was raised without the language, even though, especially my mother, she couldn't speak any English until she was fourteen-years-old. But anyway, I wanted that.

On the one hand, Native Americans may engage in inwardly directed internal oppression (Poupart, 2003), where the hatred is directed toward themselves and their intrinsic Native American identity. Participants in this study often related stories of how the constant cultural emphasis on their Indianness—and hence their presumed inferiority—whittled away at their self-image. With daily reminders, they come to believe that they *are* the stereotype with which they are being presented. The result is that "the violence, having been turned inward, becomes a toxic and effective self-loathing, culturally and individually. Can there be a more elegant violence than this?" (Neu and Therrien, 2003:4). For one Native American woman from Arizona, it was the boarding-school experience that perpetuated this acceptance of white definitions of value:

The darker you are, then they'll have nothing to do with you. So I was told that, and back in Utah, when I went to school in Utah, I was told, I'd go home for the summer every year, we got back in August. We were all dark, we spent the summer here in the sun, and one of the teachers said, "Gosh, you must have been really bad this summer." And we asked why. "Because you're darker." I mean, the more time in the sun, the darker you get, it's not like you go around doing bad things and then get darker, we were told that. And we believed it. The . . . darker you get, the more sinful, and little things like that. But it's all those little things that build up, right?

For a Colorado man, it was the public school and related peer-group experiences that conditioned his self-hatred:

There were many days I got off the bus, you know, I was bleeding, I was black and blue, I was full of knots, I was crying, you know. I'd just get all beat to hell on the bus, and you know, with all the racial slurs, you know—"You dumb, dirty, stupid, Indian." Well, let me tell you, if somebody does that to you long enough, you start to question yourself, you start to wonder, "God, is there really something to it?" And it's reinforced all kinds of ways. Yeah, they reinforce it with their fists and their feet and their brass knuckles and their book bags, and all that. But, you know, also reinforce[ed] in walking down the hall, and there's a group of them kind of coming toward you on the same side of the hall, and they immediately go all the way over to the other side, or, you know, they turn and go somewhere else, or something like that.

These stories show that the imposition of white Western perceptions of Native Americans' worth begins at a very young age. It is a relentless process that is orchestrated through the media, school curricula, and the harassment and name-calling by powerful Others such as nonnative teachers and peers. Previously I argued that this creates a situation in which victims may retaliate against their oppressors. But,

the violence, oh the violence. We've found that there isn't, there really isn't a lot of violence by white people against Native people. What we found is that there's a lot of violence by Native people against Native people. It's like they can't stand them[selves]. (Wisconsin, female)

As this woman implies, another option is to engage in outwardly directed internal oppression (Poupart, 2003). In this context, self-hatred is directed toward like Others, rather than the self. Commonly, this takes the form of family and intimate violence (Poupart, 2002, 2003; A. Smith, 2005; Bubar and Jumper-Thurman, 2004). History has many lessons to teach a people, and violence is one of them:

This is probably not a very good thing to say, but I think we've learned a lot of negative things in our own communities, learned from the white world. I think also the way we raise our children, we learned from the missionaries—the strictness, the violence, the regimentation. As communities, we're struggling with this. A lot of the violence has become internalized. I think our young men in particular fall victim to this. (Wisconsin, male)

This is a unique brand of hate crime, one that is not directed toward the differentiated Other, but the like Other. Just as interracial violence is a reflection of hostility toward those claiming American Indian identity, so, too, is this intraracial violence:

If you're a young man and you're disgusted with your surroundings and your opportunities, and you've been told you're a child that . . . that you're lesser than, I mean, you're going to feel it even more, except you go out there and inflict pain or inflict upon someone else of your own race. So it's a negative self-image that people have. And that's one of the things that always puzzled me in native communities is, you know, how we treat one another. Sometimes it just amazes me, that negativity. Negativity is just overwhelming. How Native people treat one another, they're not supposed to. (Arizona, male)

Typically, hate crime perpetrated by white people has as one of its objectives the assertion of racial superiority. Often it is intended as a punishment for racial transgression, or simply for being "raced." In the case of Indian-on-Indian violence, the latter comes to the fore. The victim is punished for reminding the perpetrator of their shared, discredited identity. To the extent that the perpetrator sees him/herself in the victim, they share the guilt of being Indian, and thus inferior, weak, perhaps less than human. The logic is defined by a disturbing parallel to white motives for anti-Indian violence. Both sets of perpetrators carry with them disparaging, and thus legitimating images of Indianness.

Not surprisingly, as this chapter has shown, many of the reactions to the normative violence described by Native Americans are negative. That is, they are characterized by withdrawal, anger, or even retaliation. Alternately, one possibility is that the ongoing incidence of hate crime can act as a catalyst to *positive* change. Frequently, those most affected by the patterns of harassment and violence resist their biographies and find strength, rather than adversity, in their identities. While anger and resentment are understandable, the opposite is also possible, that is, those who have experienced hate violence can and do develop a sense of defiance and ultimately pride in their identity. Yet defiance need not culminate only in the type of reactionary antiwhite sentiment previously noted. Rather, it may take a constructive form, by which one stands up to the racism and violence that confronts oneself.

Whether individually or collectively, there is value in challenging hate crime and the racism that informs it. Given the evidence of positive, constructive mobilization that I have gathered, I am more optimistic than many of those I cited earlier who spoke of their belief that nothing would ever change. I turn now to the final chapter, in which I highlight these progressive strategies for harnessing the energy of vibrant American Indian communities to counteract both the potential for, and the impact of, hate crime.

8
Responding to Anti-Indian Violence

Individual Responses

There is a tendency to think that social change can be initiated only through collective movements. As chapters 6 and 7 indicated, racism, violence, and their effects are pervasive and daunting. Consequently, "It may appear that individuals are powerless to stop injustice" (Weisheit and Morn, 2004:183). However this denies the viability and the importance of people acting on their principles to alter at least their own environment, and perhaps that of others at the same time. Among the participants in my study, there were many who found the courage to directly confront the racism and violence that permeated their world:

> Gallup is worse, because you can feel the stares, and me, myself, I don't take these things laying down. If I see someone looking at me that I know is thinking, "What are you doing with this Anglo?" I speak right away—"What the hell you looking at, boy, you're damn right I'm an Indian." You know, I'm not going to take this sitting down anymore, 'cause I've had incidences where I've been called a "damn prairie nigger," "chief," "blanket ass." I've been called all these things, and I've taken it, I never said anything back, you know? That's over now—I'm not gonna take it. (New Mexico, male)

As in the movie *Network*, this man and others like him recognized that there comes a time when you must shout, "I'm mad as hell and I'm not going to take it anymore!" The louder one shouts, the stronger the message sent, to both the oppressed and the oppressors, that the limit of tolerance has been reached.

Such responses are remarkably empowering for the person. They lend a sense of control in situations that might otherwise be demeaning or disabling. The ability to stand up to one's tormenter leaves an impression of strength in the face of attempts to subjugate. And it renders the tormenter impotent when he sees that the intended target will not be cowed. His hostility is repaid with a steadfast refusal to be put down or put upon.

In the context of hate crime, one function that can be attained through individual action is to directly challenge the stereotypes that underlie the violence. This is an opportunity to refuse the mask that is imposed by white culture, to reveal the diversity of Native Americans, and the sameness of Natives and nonnatives; it can play an educative role for the harasser, as in the following case drawn from the campus hate-crime survey:

> The first incident was in a class with a professor who did not know I was Native American and made some condescending remarks about Native Americans. I immediately raised my hand and told him that I had a 4.0 GPA, was in the honors program, never drank, smoked, or had sex, and I did not appreciate his stereotype. That was the only comment he ever made. (Arizona, female)

This young woman refused to allow the ignorant reference to age-old stereotypes pass. Rather, she used her biography to refute the statements, apparently with the intended effect of at least changing the offender's behavior, if not his beliefs. In short, she narrowed the perceived gap between the outdated stereotypes and the lived reality of Native Americans like herself.

Other examples of people standing up to and correcting bigotry were plentiful. A particularly memorable one occurred on a bus trip during the time of the spearfishing conflict in Wisconsin—a period of time when the truth was in short supply:

> This lady was sitting [behind] the bus driver, and I was sitting in the other front seat. And they started to talk about things, and the subject of spearing came up, and about all those fish that are thrown in the dump, and why do they take them. And he was kinda half agreeing with her. After they got through talking, I said, "Can I interject something here?" And I told them, "I don't know if people realize it or not, but those aren't fish that are thrown in the dump. It's the hide and the skeleton of the fish. The meat is taken out of it." "Oh," he says, and she didn't say nothin'. She got off in Minocqua. It's all these misconceptions and lies—they're just ignorant. (Wisconsin, female)

Again, the tables are turned in this illustration. It is not the American Indian who is silenced, but the putative offender. Correcting the inaccurate perceptions appears to have gone some distance in diminishing the power of the speaker. Others recognized the value of challenging misconceptions:

> Yeah, and that's why those actions, 'cause we take them on an individual basis to bridge the gap, as you said, that is, for individuals even, to stand up, individually or collectively, and say, "We're not the stereotype." You know, that is only a stereotype, that is only a generalization, and that we have, the majority of us have things to share with you, and things that you can learn from. (New Mexico, female)

The key here is to be ever vigilant of incidents of racism and racist violence, to challenge it directly, and to ensure that it is not allowed to flourish through complacency.

Granted, these examples involve individuals taking a stand in specific situations. But they need not be atomistic, isolated events bereft of broader significance. Individual empowerment has the potential to grow and flourish, to create a collective sense of possibility. In part, it can represent a form of modeling, signaling behaviors that others can emulate. A mother in Colorado tells this tale:

> I had this experience where me and my daughters went down for something down there, and I asked this gentlemen, you know, he had the "manager" on his little tag, and I go, "Excuse me, can we have some help here?" He just went right by, and it's like, "Hello?" And he wouldn't even acknowledge me. And they thought it was so funny, and I said, "It's not funny, girls, stop laughing." And he met this other lady that was coming down the aisle, and he met the lady and started helping her, and I knew he heard me loud and clear, and my daughters just brushed it off. I didn't want them to think that this is okay, so I got right in his face. I said, "I am a customer here, and I won't be ignored. Your job is to assist me whether I'm white, red, or orange. Now help me find what I'm looking for." That got his attention. And I taught my girls something, I think.

This is a powerful illustration of how the momentum can begin. One person challenging racism, with witnesses, can engender the repetition of similar behavior. Just as racism and its attendant violence are cumulative in their impact, so, too, is antiracism. Social movements often begin with single acts of defiance. For example, it is only a slight exaggeration to say that Rosa Parks stood her ground and ignited a movement that changed the nation. While the examples provided here are not likely to have that kind of impact, they nonetheless shape attitudes and behaviors one person at a time. The connection between the individual and the collective is noted by a woman from New Mexico:

> I'm just one of those people who are not a victim. I think that's also an important thing that individuals can do, and then it becomes a collective movement as well, just to say, "I'm not going to take it." You don't have to come across as being aggressive, just in terms of being more assertive, and not going to passive, because that doesn't help anything, that doesn't solve anything. And if you're assertive and you tell people about things, or whatever, you're educating them. Then they could say, "I didn't know that," and ignorance may be the thing, they just don't know, and now they do, and it helps them out.

There will always be a place for individual acts that challenge the contexts in which racial violence occurs. This plays largely an educative role. It becomes especially powerful in communities where formal education offers corresponding challenges to historical stereotypes and and to the invisibility of Native Americans.

Education

More than any other strategy, participants in this study stressed the importance of education in challenging racism and racist violence:

> Education—I think we need to shift a gear, make a response, become attuned to the fact that we haven't done enough. The stories need to be told—our stories, our histories, from our perspective. They forgot about the residential schools here in America. They forgot about Indian children that were stolen from Indian reservations and that didn't come home and are dead out there or were killed out there. We need to remind them that Indians came first, that they have a history, stories. (Wisconsin, male)

In chapter 4, I argued that school curricula did not do justice to the historical and contemporary place of American Indians in the United States. The colonial model of education was described as a one-way street that reflects the paradigms of cultural imperialism. Native Americans learn white culture, history, and beliefs, but neither they nor their non-native peers learn a great deal about the parallel dimensions of American

Indian lifeways. Recognizing this, many Native Americans with whom I spoke were in favor of a reinvented educational system:

> They need to listen to us, hear us. We know our culture best; we know how to tell our stories. I get so angry when they bring in all these people to teach *our* children about *ourselves*. Why can't [our] teachers do that? Let us decide what to teach, how to teach it. (Utah, female)

For many, the corrective to historically embedded colonized education must be the opposite: decolonization (Noriega, 1992; Perley, 1993). This involves an array of inclusive and participatory practices, of which the following are paramount: "recruitment of teachers, specialists, and professionals of Aboriginal background; creation (not adaptation) of a curriculum that promotes the Aboriginal cultures; recognizing and legitimizing Aboriginal histories, languages, and learning styles; and the real incorporation of Aboriginal parents in participating in the education of their children" (Perley, 1993:125–126). In pockets, many of these practices have been implemented. I spoke with several parents, for example, who were very active in the schools, offering not just linguistic and cultural insight but also role models for bridging tradition with modern Western demands:

> So there's a lot of sort of harassment of Indian kids, other kids fighting with them, that stuff, but they won't, they don't, sort of. . . . And we decided the best way was to go to the schools, to show all the kids what our culture is like, how we think, where we've been. I go into classes, I go in after school and do things with the kids—not just Indian kids. I guess I want them to see Indians as special and as the same. (Minnesota, male)

> Yeah, you know, I actually wanted to help. I work with racism in schools. That's where it all starts. And if we can capture some of these families, through their kids, that could be an anchorage in the culture. That's what I did all my life, go to the schools. It was really interesting for me, but anyway, that's all what I do with kids. And for white kids, too, right? You know, get them through the ignorance that they got from home. Like you say, they've got some of the culture and language in, but that's just people coming in occasionally. I try to go in every week so they see me as a real person, not somebody from a Western movie. (Utah, male)

Additionally, many of the reservation schools, in particular, had very high proportions of Native American teachers and administrators. One teacher shared her biography:

> My parents came through the boarding schools, with a lot of scars you don't see but that don't heal. They wouldn't, I guess couldn't, give me our culture or language. It had been scared out of them. It was what that did to them. So I did what I could to get it back—talked to elders, took language classes, went to school. That's why I wanted to teach back here, so these kids can get back their roots, their histories. (Arizona, female)

It is this deep understanding and commitment that will facilitate a different kind of education, one that recognizes the harm that has been done to Native American youth in the name of colonized education in the past. It is in this context of authenticity that the integration of Native American curricula will be most successful. The adoption of this approach appears to be uneven across the communities that I visited. In some, the perception was that not enough was being done, that there was a need for more extensive teaching of Native American issues: "No, there doesn't, and that's a shame, because, you know, my daughter said what they should do, start teaching Navajo in the first or second grade, and then start introducing the culture, so that the kids would understand, and then introduce our culture to the Navajos, do a little bit of both" (Arizona, female).

Integrating Native American curricula into the schools is but one part of what must be a broader educational strategy. Antiprejudice and antiviolence programs are also important factors to consider. These were the sort of initiatives for which many participants saw a need. There was recognition that it wasn't awareness of Native American culture alone that was needed, but that decades of deeply ingrained prejudice would also have to be combated. The intergenerational cycles of hate also require fundamental work.

> Well, educating the people, educating people on discrimination, especially the kids, they know, they know that their parents don't like certain people, or their parents don't like this guy, or this person, or, you know, they know this, the little kids know these things, and they just go along with what their parents say. So I think a lot of it has to do with education in the school system about discrimination, especially

racial and sexual discrimination, all kinds of discrimination, you know. (Arizona, male)

Projects like those intimated here have sprung up across the country, especially in elementary and secondary schools, and could easily be implemented in border-town schools. For example, the Anti-Defamation League's Stop the Hate program is a multidimensional antibias program that offers peer training to secondary-school students. Additionally, recognizing the extent to which hate crime is shaped by the broader community sentiment, Stop the Hate extends diversity training not only to teachers and school administrators but also to parents and the community. The Southern Poverty Law Center, another partner in antibias programming, has developed a similarly impressive model through its Teaching Tolerance project. This preventive initiative assists educators in designing curricula that encourage students to recognize, understand, and value difference.

A recent manual jointly published by the Department of Education and the Department of Justice, *Preventing Youth Hate Crime* (nd), identifies seven "elements of effective school-based hate prevention programs." The criteria address an array of issues, from the identification and measurement of hate crime in every school, to potential responses to hate-crime offenders. The emphasis, however, is on educational initiatives that attempt to disrupt the boundaries that separate Us from Them. The stated elements are:

1. Provide hate prevention training to all staff.
2. Ensure that all students receive hate prevention training through age-appropriate school-based activities.
3. Develop partnerships with families, community organizations, and law enforcement agencies.
4. Develop a hate prevention policy to distribute to every student, every student's family, and every employee of the school district.
5. Develop a range of corrective actions for those who violate school hate prevention policies.
6. Collect and use data to focus district-wide hate prevention efforts.
7. Provide structured opportunities for integration.

School boards in towns bordering Native American reservations, or with high concentrations of Native American students, would be well advised to consider the implementation of antihate programs modeled on these criteria. To the extent that educational activities, in the schools and in the community, are able to deconstruct damaging and divisive stereotypes, they will continue to be effective mechanisms by which to counteract prejudice and, ultimately, hate crime. While not all educators or students will be receptive to the alternative messages of tolerance, "For every school child and young adult that we can and do reach, we shall be influencing a world beyond our own" (Kleg, 1993:260).

Community Awareness

Clearly, formal educational initiatives have a role to play in the long-term historical project of correcting misconceptions about Native Americans, and of correcting the history books. However this can and should be accompanied by more informal community-based initiatives intended to similarly alter the relationship between Native and nonnative communities. A likely starting point for crossing borders might be through the process of engagement. This involves willingness on all sides to make meaningful contact, to begin to see one another anew:

> It can change the way we see, hear, think, and feel. It can propel us across vast differences in culture and experience. It can move us past our fears. When we engage, truly engage, we let go and grab on at the same time. We loose our hold on old truths even as we reach out for new ones. We sacrifice neatness for the messiness of reality and comfort for the occasional pain of honest dealing. (Dalton, 1995:27)

Dalton's assessment is not so different from that of many of the Native Americans with whom I spoke. There was a widespread recognition of the need for both Native and nonnative communities to reach across the divide that has artificially separated them. For the blinders to come off, for the masks to fall away, the distinct cultures must be drawn together. Simply by making contact, they create the potential for seeing through the stereotypes to the real character of a people:

> But I just think that it's going to take both sides of the cultures to really understand the differences. Once you do that, I think you break down a lot of those walls. If people can come over and eat mutton with us, that's the big step right there, you know? Because it seems that we've kind of taken part in most everything that the dominant

culture has to offer, but vice versa, we don't really see that the other way. (New Mexico, male)

Engagement facilitates awareness. It requires a conscious effort to interact on an immediate rather than distant plane.

There were three distinct types of community awareness initiatives suggested by participants. The first of these was often treated facetiously, despite the potentially serious impact it could have on community awareness. On at least a dozen occasions, people suggested that the American Indian community boycott the commercial centers that they typically frequented. This generally referred to nearby border towns and their grocery and department stores in particular. As I said, this suggestion was frequently offered in jest, with a metaphorical wink and a nod. Others were slightly more sincere:

> So I've always wondered about that. Say the Navajo Nation was really getting really serious about this. And say the president called for a boycott in Gallup. I wonder what kind of damage that would do to these people. I know that this is one thing that would scare the hell out of people. I was in the K-Mart yesterday, and K-Mart would definitely fall to pieces I think. It draws attention to the problems, to the issues. (New Mexico, male)

A Minnesota man recalled that such a boycott had indeed taken place in Bemidji several years ago:

> We boycotted the city. We stopped shopping. We took our money out of the banks and got the other reservation to join us. Because people thought we were dirt poor and didn't realize we had twenty-five million dollars in the banks in Bemidji, and right now it's probably, it's probably more than one hundred million dollars, you know? Easy.

The point of such initiatives is, of course, to remind the nonnative community how much they rely on Native American dollars for their own prosperity. As the last quote suggests, at the very least it breaks through the myth that American Indians have no money to spend. Rather, it reinforces the symbiotic relationship between the two communities. Native Americans need the goods and services that nearby white communities provide, but the latter also need Native American commerce for their revenue.

This is a deceptively simple way to make the point that American Indians have a vital place in the economy and society of their region. It is a creative lesson in the worth of Native Americans. However, boycotts may backfire, creating greater hostility toward the offending group. More constructive is the second suggestion: that the community engage in promotional programs, including media campaigns, promotional displays and activities, and intercultural events. The goal here is to draw the nonnative community in, to demonstrate through word and deed the strengths, the beauty, the humanity of Native American cultures. This type of initiative highlights the positive aspects of the culture, and thus cuts through the damaging stereotypes that inform hate-motivated violence; it provides opportunities to begin a dialogue between the communities.

Participants suggested an array of activities, some of which they had seen practiced, some of which they hoped to see in the future. Interestingly, one man from Minnesota suggested the use of the media as a conduit for informing the nonnative communities about events and issues in Indian Country:

> Yeah, but I think that publicly, as a community, you know, we can generate our awareness from within. One of the things that I want to do with the peace project is to begin assembling some literature, and maybe four times a year do a printing and have it inserted into a local newspaper . . . You know, and just be consistent about it, four times a year, people from Bemidji, this will be in the newspaper and you can read it or you can ignore it, but it's in front of you, it's on your breakfast table when you pick up the fish wrapper. It will generate discussion, provoke the discussion, whatever you got to do. Even if we piss somebody off, they're talking right, start that dialogue, no matter how it needs to be done.

This could very well be a useful corrective to the negative or nonexistent media representations of contemporary American Indian matters. Combine this with another frequently suggested initiative: promotional activities that highlight the positive elements of Native American culture:

> Well, maybe more promotional types of things, I've noticed that, well, the museum does a great job, they have their Native American series, you can see it on the flags outside. And the Native American

Week, that's good, maybe. I don't know, we talked years ago about having the powwows again, but, it was good. (New Mexico, female)

Yeah, and I know, I think they have their fry bread booth, the fair, and things like that. But I would like to see maybe a Native American cultural center or something like that, something where we get to showcase our talents, as far as the people within our community, and bring more people into the community, and say, "Look at this, we're somebody, we're here." (New Mexico, female)

Such events can showcase talent, thereby challenging the stereotypes of uncivilized savages. Related to these are participatory activities that are intended to engage nonnatives. Intercultural events were suggested by some as yet another way to initiate dialogue, to begin the process of crosscultural engagement:

We hold potlucks, native performers come into town, performing types of stuff at the university, you know? Embracing some real cultural things, doing more of the educational level and at the community level. Everybody's welcome, and it's not just for Indians. I'm just saying I'd like to see more of that happening, you know? You never want to be in a situation . . . where you're doing something because of an issue, reacting to problems. I mean, that's why we talk about diversity in the school here, not something [where] you just take the curriculum off the shelf and then put it back on. It's ongoing. And they're gonna be affected, because they're part of it, they're at the table with us. (Arizona, male)

The final category identified by the participants revolved around more formal "racism treatment programs," as one person humorously designated them. What is really meant here are formal training and workshop protocols that might be implemented in such settings as workplaces, local councils, and community organizations (e.g., Rotarians).

Well, we do the annual conference thing. We've got a human rights committee, we've got a diversity training committee, we go out in the schools, we've been in the private sector, law enforcement, not just in Bemidji, but the extending counties, beyond, you know?—to go in and do a workshop training on human rights and sensitivity and employment and all those things. It's kind of ongoing. We meet once a month to talk about those particular situations, a lot of intake and referrals. 'Cause that's what it's about. Like in literature, it's about being fully active and resolving what can be resolved if they want to talk. It's conflict resolution, basically, [is] what it's about. (Minnesota, male)

Criminal Justice Responses–Victim Services

It is telling that virtually no participants mentioned criminal justice initiatives by which to intervene in hate crime. Indeed, one person noted that we have extensive legislation—rights laws, etc.—but that this has not served Native Americans well thus far. In fact, it has been through legislative measures that American Indians have been displaced, assimilated, and deculturated. Thus he questions the value of criminal justice initiatives:

> You know, the disease of racism is one that public policy can only go so far in terms of correcting . . . I mean, you can only legislate and enforce up to a certain point, and I think we're, in terms of the existing civil rights law, we are all the way there. No, maybe not in terms of the law itself, okay—but I think that on the enforcement end of it, more could be done . . . It's almost like somebody has to get killed before they take a serious interest, you know? Somebody dies, and then they'll really prosecute to its fullest extent. But short of that . . . (Minnesota, male)

The consistent failure to suggest legal responses to hate crime is no doubt a reflection of the lack of trust in the criminal justice system on the part of Native peoples. It is also an accurate reflection of the historical lack of sensitivity with which the criminal justice system has responded to minority victims of crime generally. Ogawa (1999:4) succinctly describes the quandary facing victims of crime: "All victims of crime are susceptible to being mistreated by uncaring, misinformed or antagonistic individuals and/or an overburdened, ponderous and jaded criminal justice system. These are insensitivities or injustices that victims of every race and ethnicity have endured." The task of the criminal justice system, then, is to mitigate the negative effects of difference not only for communities but also for individual victims of those communities. The experience of victimization is traumatic for all people; however it can be doubly, triply so for those whose difference leaves them even more vulnerable and at the mercy of a "jaded criminal justice system."

Criminal justice agencies that are representative of the communities they serve—tribal police, for example—will almost invariably be more aware of the particular problems of these communities. However, minority groups are dramatically underrepresented as service providers in the criminal justice system. In Indian Country, this situation demands that agencies recruit Native Americans. These recruits can bring with them an understanding of their clientele, as well as slightly different approaches to their jobs. Nonetheless, hiring and promoting American Indians within criminal justice agencies is no guarantee that those agencies will necessarily be more sensitive to cultural diversity. There is some evidence to suggest that minority recruits may, in fact, treat members of their communities with the same indifference and hostility as their white counterparts (Barlow, 1994; Martin, 1994; Peak, 1997). As I showed in chapter 6, criminal justice officials are themselves perpetrators and facilitators of hate crime, as they police the boundaries of difference. Consequently, regardless of the makeup of criminal justice agencies, cultural awareness training will have a crucial role to play in sensitizing its members to the experiences, values, and needs of the communities they serve. Criminal justice practitioners must be made aware that different communities may in fact experience the trauma of victimization in different ways. A recent Office for Victims of Crime report (1998:157) observes that "different concepts of suffering and healing influence how victims experience the effects of victimization and the process of recovery ... Methods for reaching culturally diverse victims must include resources that are specific to their needs."

Bigfoot (2000) identifies an array of barriers to services that typically confront Native American victims of crime. This is the array of issues that must be corrected to effectively serve victims of hate crime as well:

- Suspicion of law enforcement including tribal and federal personnel
- Unwillingness to cooperate with investigation or prosecution
- Limited access to tribal or state victim assistance programs
- Limited infrastructure—transportation, childcare, telephone, programs and services, adequate referral source, etc.
- Limited information on services available
- Lack of community support for disclosure of victimization
- Limited tribal jurisdiction for accountability and penalties
- Limited federal jurisdiction for violations other than major crimes
- Limited economy to build an infrastructure to support programs

- Inappropriate or limited understanding of Native issues by nonnatives, and
- Acceptance of abusive and harmful relationships and criminal injury.

Awareness and knowledge of how hate crimes affect Native Americans will allow criminal justice actors to implement services that are appropriate to localized dynamics. Ultimately, the key to effective delivery of victim services is sensitivity to the cultural needs of the victim's community, in a way that empowers victims and potential victims.

Rights-based Activism

Native Americans have a role to play in empowering themselves. As noted above, this cannot be left to government. This begins with an awareness of the rights to which they are entitled—legal, political, and treaty—but then must extend to an exercise of those rights. In short, Native Americans must be educated on the nature and use of their rights:

> That would be perfect, it would be great if they would fight for their rights. I don't know, no one wants to stick their neck out—the whole thing is, you put your hand out, and it's either going to get bitten or shaken. If bitten, try again, because it'll be all right. Listen, I don't know if it was really different in the fifties, things were relatively segregated, they didn't even think about it. (Arizona, female)

> Yeah, and that's how I learned that it was better to do that than to try and fight city hall. So a good part of my life has been exactly that, but as I grew older, as I went into the military and came out, that was when I realized that there was a need to speak out, there was a need, for me especially, for me to stand my ground, you know. I wasn't going to be told, and I started coming out. I felt that there was a need, because prior to that there wasn't enough of the Navajo people who were educated enough to get into, to get the message out, and a lot of them did it, and we needed to start communicating with the leaders on the outside, the communities, so that they can better understand us, and we can better understand them. (Arizona, male)

The structure of rights in the United States allows for multiple sites of contestation for Native Americans. In the past, individuals and tribes have asserted their claims to legal rights, religious rights, political rights, and, of course, treaty rights. The wide array of putative rights, then, provides some impetus for collective mobilization around individual rights, as well as broader struggles for collective and social rights. The outstanding feature that the most successful approaches share is that they have not restricted their political activities to the field of rights litigation. Their rights claims took on a number of expressions, including congressional lobbying, extended research, public demonstrations, and public education, all in an attempt to construct a transformative politics of identity. This is vital. If oppositional activity was restricted to rights litigation, it would contribute to a narrow legalization of politics. But the politics of rights is not and should not be so confined: "We are more likely to arrive at a positive conception of rights strategies if we see them as part of the wider field of hegemonic political practices. Whilst rights-in-isolation may be of limited utility, rights as a significant component of counter-hegemonic strategies provide a potentially fruitful approach to the prosecution of transformatory political practice" (Hunt, 1990:18). The key to progressive political transformation is not to rely solely on legal battles around rights. Rights litigation must become part of a comprehensive strategy that absorbs and supersedes the liberal hegemonic formation; in short, it is necessary to engage in counterhegemonic strategies. And in fact, such activism has been apparent in the communities that I visited.

In chapter 7, the point was made that ongoing racial harassment and violence can be debilitating. It oppresses, it defeats, it embitters. Yet as the opening section of this chapter illustrates, the same patterns can motivate constructive responses. Earlier I spoke of individual acts of constructive defiance. Here I turn to the potential for violence to collectively mobilize a community in defense. This was the case in New York City, for example, where Haitians accompanied by other Caribbeans demonstrated angrily, vocally, and visibly against the racist violence represented by Abner Louima's brutal beating at the hands of police officers in 1997. While innumerable victims had previously remained silent out of fear and intimidation, the publicity surrounding Louima's victimization galvanized the community into action. A decade earlier, other New York neighborhoods witnessed similar rallies. The racially motivated murders of Michael Griffith in Howard Beach in 1996 and Yusuf Hawkins in Bensonhurst in 1989 both resulted in flurries of organizing and demonstrating. An organization created after the first murder, New York City Civil Rights Coalition, was still available to lend its support to those involved in prosecuting the Hawkins case. Both incidents inspired widespread demonstrations condemning the racism of the perpetrators' communities, as well as the racist culture of New York City generally. Clearly these cases stimulated, rather than disabled, the communities. And from the observations of participants in these studies, there is ample evidence that anti-Indian activity has had the unintended effect of inspiring similar mobilization across American Indian communities. Isolated as well as ongoing patterns of racial discrimination and violence can and do trigger community-based reactions in the interests of racial justice.

The strength and resilience of Native Americans in the face of the everyday violence described here is remarkable. In fact, they currently enjoy a resurgence of numbers and nationalist identity. As Frideres (1993:508) puts it, "With the emergence of Native identity, the sense of alienation experienced by many Natives has been dispelled by a new sense of significance and purpose." The activism that has been at the root of so much violence, and the backlash associated with it, has engendered a renewed pride in American Indian identity, and with it, a recognition of the need to pursue that which is theirs by right. In short, it has mobilized Native Americans around their cultural identity and political sovereignty.

> A lot of people—this has been my experience anyway—even among Indian people there were people saying "Don't!" Because when you're told you're bad for doing something, and told a thousand times, sometimes you start to believe is. And there were others that weren't quite sure but became supportive. People who don't go to meetings were coming to meetings. People who went about their lives, they wanted, they really needed to learn what are these treaties [are] about, how did they occur, you know? And they developed the sense that it was a birthright for future generations. That was exciting. That was a very positive outcome of the conflict, that will have contributions for years to come. (Wisconsin, male)

It is these sorts of reactions to the normativity of violence that will ultimately present the greatest defense. To use the moment of victimization to confront and challenge oppression speaks volumes. In particular, it says to the perpetrator that Native Americans refuse to stay in their place but will instead fight for a reconstructed definition of what that place is.

Moreover, such resistance also sends a powerful message of strength and solidarity to American Indian communities as well.

> And it's true because there has been a rebirth, a resurgence of pride, finally, again, in native culture. To me, it's sort of ironic that there's some value to be found in the reactionary treaty vows, because that has drawn so many people back to their homeland and back to their tradition, you know? It's sort of protecting, coming back from to protect the community and becoming a part of it again. And so it's a horrible twist of fate to those who would like to see the culture eliminated. That was their goal in engaging in this violence, was to silence those uppity Indians in Wisconsin, or in Washington, and it had exactly the opposite effect. And it's just wonderful to watch, to see that that's happened. (Arizona, female)

The recent history of activism has had a remarkably positive impact, not just on the material reality of American Indians but also on their sense of empowerment. The effects are hoped by some to be long-term, intergenerational, and not restricted solely to those engaged in the various struggles:

> I see it going in the positive sense, when I think that what the tribe was, the crossroads they've come to. I see it as being very good. What they are trying to do is create in this upcoming generation, certainly planning for the generation to follow, an understanding. Regaining of some of their old cultural values which include the language itself. They are trying to reteach the language. Their philosophies, their religions things, like that—trying to rekindle that into this generation to follow, and certain ones in the future, and at the same time blend that with the many positive ways to live in today's society with other people. They want to come out of the past and into the present by retaining some of the past and forging ahead into the future . . . And I see their philosophies changing. It incorporates life with other communities. (Wisconsin, female)

What is encouraging here is the optimism that American Indian nations can change and are changing in ways that will ensure their strength and viability in the long term.

We see here that strategies of transformative politics are already part of the arsenal of many Native American communities. But such strategists must recognize the need to extend both the discourse and the object of struggle, to not be constrained by state definitions of rights (Korsmo, 1999). A radical, participatory democracy must include the social, economic, and collective rights that are the prerequisites for the exploitation of the liberal political and civil rights enshrined in such documents as the Bill of Rights. However, this does not go far enough. Recall that it is the structural elements of oppression that condition the environment for hate crime to emerge. Consequently, rights struggles must also include transformations in the political economy of Native American communities, thereby making the attainment of substantial equality and freedom a genuine possibility.

Rights claims have significant implications for counterhegemonic strategies. Such strategies would involve the exploitation of the logic-of-rights discourse to transcend the specifically liberal form of the rights as defined by the state. One area, in particular, that has increasingly come to the fore among indigenous peoples worldwide has been the collective rights of self-determination and self-government.

Toward Self-determination

We know that in order to protect and preserve our cultural identity we must continue to exercise our rights to self-determination to the fullest extent possible. The social, political and economic injustices on this reservation [and others] will subside only after we have addressed them . . . we are merely exercising our rights as a nation, in hopes of maintaining our homelands and traditions through effective self-governance. (Friedlander-Shelby, 1989, online)

The ethnic renewal noted above provides a point of departure for more self-conscious mobilization around structural reform aimed at decolonization. Such strategies must be located at the crucial sites that have reinforced the structural exclusion and disempowerment of Native American individuals and communities. They must be initiated and played out by the American Indian community. Abdicating responsibility for countering such institutional practices, and their associated violence, to the state will not be a sufficiently effective long-term strategy. First of all, it has been federal and provincial policy that has largely left Native Americans bereft of institutionalized power. Second, the last decade of the twentieth century has seen a flurry of hate-crime legislation and other state activities, none of which have had an appreciable effect on the frequency or certainly the severity of hate crime. Such initiatives are insufficient responses to bias-motivated violence, in that they do not touch the underlying structures that support hate crime. The ultimate goal is not only to attack hate crime but also to disrupt the institutional and cultural assumptions about difference that conditions hate crime.

One of the themes underlying my conceptualization of hate crime is that it is legitimated and accompanied by an array of facilitative mechanisms, such as stereotypes, language, legislation, and job segregation. It is apparent, for example, that stereotyping Native Americans as savages, or criminalizing their rituals, or excluding them from citizenship, have served to maintain their stigmatized outsider identity.

Nonetheless, there is reason for hope. To the extent that difference is socially constructed, it can also be socially reconstructed. As a society, we can redefine the ways in which difference matters. We can strive for a just and democratic society, in which the full spectrum of diversity is reevaluated in a positive and celebratory light.

And so an insurgent politics of difference must reconstruct both the cultural and institutional supports for particular ways of doing and valuing difference:

> Yeah, you talk about the coalition now, and other things that are going on, . . . there's a social economic injustice in this town, and you don't have the tools, we need to get to that point, talk about social justice, talk about economics. Well, let's talk about welfare, insurance, housing, and everything, yeah, especially employment. And the high unemployment. But they'll tell you, politicians will tell you different. I think it's run about 60-some percent, but I tell tribal chiefs here that it's higher than that. (Minnesota, female)

Such changes, of course, will not occur magically or out of the beneficence of the state or some imagined hegemonic bloc. On the contrary, they will require the concentrated efforts of grassroots mobilizations. The new social movements, including Native American rights movement, that have done the transformative labor of the last half of the twentieth century must continue to extend the early gains in the workplace, in the home, and in the public imagination.

We would do well to heed Young's (1990) advice that we embrace a positive politics of difference. This would involve much more than efforts to assimilate Others, or merely tolerate their presence. We have seen what assimilationist policies have wrought in the lives of American Indians. Rather, it challenges us to celebrate our differences. Of course, this requires that much of our current way of ordering the world would be radically altered. It means that we must cease to define difference as inferior, and see it instead as simply not the same. As Minow (1990:377) states so elegantly, "Changing the ways we classify, evaluate, reward, and punish may make the differences we had noticed less significant . . . irrelevant or even a strength. The way things are is not the only way things could be." This is "doing difference" differently, under different ground rules, where enacting one's identity is not an occasion for potential rebuke. Rather, doing difference becomes a risk-free expression of one's culture, perspectives, and insights. In achieving these ends, the foundations that support hate violence will be weakened, so that such violence becomes anomalous, rather than normative, as it has been described herein.

A related element of the agenda of structural reform is decolonization, or the assertion of self-determination. The contemporary sovereigntist discourses can be traced to the social activism of the 1960s, during which emerging American Indian movements made the claim for self-determination over assimilation, and by which they intended "the right to assume control of their own lives independent of federal control, the creation of conditions for a new era in which the Indian future would be determined by Indian acts and Indian decisions, and the assurance that Indian people would not be separated involuntarily from their tribal groups" (Johnson, Champagne, and Nagel, 1997:14). These guiding principles remain part of the Native sovereignty movement to this day.

The question of sovereignty is directly relevant to hate crime. One of the greatest challenges in protecting Native Americans from racialized violence perpetrated by nonnatives lies in the law itself. The 1978 Oliphant Decision, in particular, renders Native American victimization at the hands of nonnatives jurisdictionally problematic, while at the same time also represents a lasting challenge to Native American self-governance.

The Oliphant Decision revolved around the application of the Suquamish tribe's Law and Order Code to two cases involving white offenders. In a devastating blow, the Supreme Court ruled that tribal courts had no jurisdiction over nonnative offenders. In the context of hate crime, the decision would seem to imply that Native Americans have little legal recourse to protect themselves from white hate-crime offenders. State, or more likely, federal authorities could, of course, be called in. However, given the relatively minor nature of most race-based incidents, the state and the FBI have limited interest in pursuing such cases. The broader issue raised by Oliphant, however, concerns the very question of Indian self-determination. The decision eroded tribes' abilities to police their own territory. It represented, to many Native Americans, yet another effort to redefine tribes not as sovereign nations but as dependent states whose powers should be thus constrained. It is but one among many pieces of legal machinery that must be dismantled in the interests of Native American self-determination.

Simply stated, "Indigenous peoples have the right of self-determination. By virtue of that right, they freely determine their political status and freely pursue their economic, social and cultural development" (Article 3, draft United Nations Declaration on the Rights of Indigenous Peoples). Article 31 goes even further, articulating the areas in which self-determination should prevail:

> Indigenous peoples, as a specific form of exercising their right to self-determination, have the right to autonomy or self-government in matters relating to their internal and local affairs, including culture, religion, education, information, media, health, housing, employment, social welfare, economic activities, land and resource management, environment, and entry by non-members, as well as ways and means for financing these autonomous functions.

Native peoples' involvement in decisions affecting their economies, cultures, and environments is paramount to fundamentally altering their circumstances. Grassroots organizing and decision making will reflect the daily realities that currently leave them vulnerable to hate crime. Who better to determine what employment opportunities are needed, or what political structures will facilitate democratization in Indian Country? Self-guided action plans for economic and social development, in keeping with American Indian and not Euroamerican values, will enable progress that is sensitive to the specific needs of Native American communities. Both the processes and outcomes contribute to the empowerment of Indian people and nations.

The histories and identities of Native Americans are unique among minority groups in the United States; consequently, the future of overcoming the legacy of ethnocide and ethnoviolence must also be culturally specific. The unique strength from which Native Americans might draw is the existence of tribal political entities across the nation, and in fact, crossing international boundaries, into Canada, Mexico, and beyond. Aboriginal people across the globe are experiencing similar causes and manifestations of structural and physical racial violence, and are mobilizing against them (Quesenberry, 1999; Cuneen, 2001). The key, then, is a collective, rather than localized, mobilization of political will. Just as the anti-Indian movement has been able to muster a collective voice, so, too, can Native American communities react strategically on a national and global level to demand enforcement of hate-crime and civil-rights legislation, to educate against bigotry, to engage in campaigns against the institutions and mythologies that shape ethnoviolence. At base, this must be part of the broader agenda toward Native sovereignty.

Bibliography

Adams, D. (1995). *Education for extinction: American Indians and the boarding school experience, 1875–1928.* Lawrence, Kans.: University Press of Kansas.

Allen, P. G. (1986). *Sacred hoop.* Boston: Beacon Press.

Bachman, R. (1992). *Death and violence on the reservation.* New York: Auburn House.

Barker, R. (1992). *The broken circle.* New York: Simon and Schuster.

Barlow, D. (1994). Minorities policing minorities as a strategy of social control: A historical analysis of tribal police in the United States. *Criminal Justice History*, 15: 141–163.

Barnes, A. (2000). *Everyday racism.* Naperville, Ill.: Sourcebooks, Inc.

Beauvais, F. (1996). Trends in Indian adolescent drug and alcohol use. In M. Nielsen and R. Silverman (eds.), *Native Americans, crime and justice* (pp. 89–95). Boulder, Colo.: Westview.

Beck, D. (1995). From colonization to self-determination: American Indian higher education before 1974. In *Critical Issues in American Indian Higher Education.* Chicago: NAES College.

Bensen, R. (2001). *Children of the Dragonfly: Native American voices on child custody and education.* Tucson, Ariz.: University of Arizona Press.

Berrill, K., and Herek, G. (1992). Anti-gay violence and victimization in the United States. In G. Herek and K. Berrill (eds.), *Hate crime: Confronting violence against lesbians and gay men* (pp. 19–45). Thousand Oaks, Calif.: Sage.

Bigfoot, D. S. (2000). *History of victimization in native communities.* Oklahoma City, Okla.: Center on Child Abuse and Neglect.

Boldt, M. (1993). *Surviving as Indians: The challenge of self-government.* Toronto, Ontario: University of Toronto Press.

Bonilla-Silva, E. (1999). The new racism: Racial structure in the United States. In P. Wong (ed.), *Race, ethnicity, and nationality in the United States* (pp. 55–101). Boulder, Colo.: Westview.

Bordewich, F. (1996). *Killing the white man's indian: Reinventing Native Americans at the end of the twentieth century.* New York: Doubleday.

Bowling, B. (1993). Racial harassment and the process of victimization. *British Journal of Criminology*, 33(2), 231–250.

Bowling, B. (1998). *Violent racism: Victimisation, policing and social context.* Oxford, UK: Oxford University Press.

Brownmiller, S. (1974). *Against our will*. New York: Simon and Schuster.

Bubar, R., and Jumper-Thurman, P. (2004). Violence against native women. *Social Justice, 31*(4), 70–86.

Bunch, C. (1995). Transforming human rights from a feminist perspective. In C. Bunch (ed.), *Women's rights, human rights* (pp. 11–16). New York: Routledge.

Butler, J. (1993). Endangered/endangering: Schematic racism and white paranoia. In R. Gooding-Williams (ed.), *Reading Rodney King, reading urban uprisings* (pp. 15–22). New York: Routledge.

Canada, Department of Justice. (1991). *Aboriginal people and justice administration: A discussion paper*. Ottawa, Ontario: Department of Justice.

Carlson, D. (1997). Stories of colonial and post-colonial education. In M. Fine, L. Weis, L. Powell, and L. Mun Wong (eds.), *Off white: Readings on race, power and society* (pp. 137–148). New York: Routledge.

Carney, C. (1999). *Native American higher education in the United States*. New Brunswick, N.J.: Transaction.

Carpio, M. (2004). The lost generation: American Indian women and sterilization abuse. *Social Justice, 31*(4), 40–53.

Champagne, D. (1998). American Indian studies is for everyone. In D. Mihesuah (ed.), *Natives and academics: Researching and writing about American Indians* (pp. 181–189). Lincoln, Nebr.: University of Nebraska Press.

Churchill, W. (1992). The earth is our mother: Struggle for American Indian land and liberation in the contemporary United States. In A. Jaimes (ed.), *The state of Native America* (pp. 217–240). Boston: South End Press.

Churchill, W. (1994). *Indians are us?* Monroe, Maine: Common Courage Press.

Churchill, W., and W. LaDuke. (1992). Native North America: The political economy of radioactive colonialism. In A. Jaimes (ed.), *The state of Native America* (pp. 241–266). Boston: South End Press.

Churchill, W., and Vander Wall, J. (1990). *Agents of repression*. Boston: South End Press.

Cook, J. (1992). Collection and analysis of hate crime activities. In R. Kelly (ed.), *Bias crime: American law enforcement and legal responses* (pp. 143–150). Chicago: Office of International Criminal Justice.

Cook, N. D. (1998). *Born to die*. Cambridge, N.Y.: Cambridge University Press.

Crow Dog, M. (1990). *Lakota woman*. New York: Harper Perennial.

Crump, J. (2004). Producing and enforcing the geography of hate: Race, housing segregation, and housing-related hate crimes in the United States. In C. Flint (ed.), *Spaces of hate: Geographies of discrimination and intolerance in the U.S.* (pp. 227–244). New York: Routledge.

Cuneen, C. (2001). *Conflict, politics and crime: Aboriginal communities and the police*. Crow's Nest, NSW, Australia: Allen and Unwin.

Dalton, H. (1995). *Racial healing: Confronting the fear between blacks and whites*. New York: Doubleday.

Dekeseredy, W., Alvi, S., Schwartz, M., and Tomaszewski, A. (2002). *Under siege: Poverty and crime in a public housing community.* Lanham, Md.: Lexington Books.

Deyhle, D., and Swisher, K. (1997). Research in American Indian and Alaskan Native education: From assimilation to self-determination. In M. Apple (ed.), *Review of research in education* (vol. 22, pp. 113–194). Washington, D.C.: American Educational Research Association.

Dumont, J. (1996). Justice and native peoples. In M. Nielsen and R. Silverman (eds.), *Native Americans, crime and justice* (pp. 20–33). Boulder, Colo.: Westview.

Duran, E., and Duran, B. (1995). *Native American post-colonial psychology.* Albany, N.Y.: State University of New York Press.

Ehrlich, H. (1998). Prejudice and ethnoviolence on campus. *Higher Education Extension Service Review, 6*(2), 1–13.

Ehrlich, H. (1999). Campus ethnoviolence. In F. Pincus and H. Ehrlich (eds.), *Ethnic conflict* (pp. 277–290). Boulder Colo.: Westview.

Faery, R. (1999). *Cartographies of desire: Captivity, race and sex in the shaping of an American Nation.* Norman, Okla.: University of Oklahoma Press.

Fanon, F. (2000). The fact of blackness. In L. Back and J. Solomos (eds.), *Theories of race and racism* (pp. 257–266). London: Routledge.

Feagin, J. (2001). *Racist America: Roots, current realities and future reparations.* New York: Routledge.

Federal Bureau of Investigation (2005). *Hate crime statistics, 2004.*

Fine, M., Weis, L., and Addelston, J. (1997). (In)Secure times: Constructing white working class masculinities in the late twentieth century. *Gender and Society, 11*(1), 52–68.

Fixico, D. (1998). *The invasion of Indian country in the twentieth century: American capitalism and tribal natural resources.* Boulder, Colo.: University Press of Colorado.

Fixico, D. (2000). *The urban indian experience in America.* Albuquerque, N. Mex.: University of New Mexico Press.

Forbes, J. (1991). Envelopment, proletarianization and inferiorization: Aspects of colonialism. *Journal of Ethnic Studies, 18*(4), 95–122.

Fournier, S., and Crey, E. (1997). *Stolen from our embrace: The abduction of First Nations children and restoration of aboriginal communities.* Vancouver, British Columbia: Douglas and McIntyre.

Freire, P. (1970). *Pedagogy of the oppressed.* New York: Continuum Publishing Company.

Frideres, J. (1993). *Native peoples in Canada: Contemporary conflicts.* Scarborough, Ontario: Prentice Hall.

Friedlander-Shelby, V. (1989). *Racism on the Flathead Reservation: A correlation of the Confederated Salish and Kootenai Tribes' ability to effectively self-govern.*

Center for World Indigenous Studies. Retrieved November 5, 2007, from www.cwis.org/fwdp/Americas/flathead.txt.

Frye, M. (2004). Oppression. In P. Rothenberg (ed.), *Race, class and gender in the United States* (6th ed., pp. 174–178). New York: Worth Publishers.

Gedicks, A. (1991). *Racism and resource colonization in ceded territory of the Wisconsin Chippewa*. Paper presented to the American Indian History and Culture Conference, Green Bay, Wisconsin.

General Accounting Office (1976). *Investigation of allegations concerning Indian health services* B-164031(5): HRD-77–3. Washington, D.C.: General Accounting Office.

Georges-Abeyie, D. (1990). The myth of a racist criminal justice system? In B. MacLean and D. Milovanovic (eds.), *Racism, empiricism and criminal justice*. Vancouver, British Columbia: Collective Press.

Georges-Abeyie, D. (2001). Foreword: Petit apartheid in criminal justice: "The More 'Things' Change, the More 'Things' Remain the Same." In D. Milovanovic and K. Russell (eds.), *Petit apartheid in the U.S. criminal justice system* (ix–xiv). Durham, N.C.: Carolina Academic Press.

Goldberg, D. (1993). *Racist culture*. Oxford, United Kingdom: Oxford University Press.

Grenier, L. (1998). *Working with indigenous knowledge*. Ottawa, Ontario: International Development Research Center.

Grossman, Z. (1999). *Treaty rights and responding to anti-Indian activity*. Center for World Indigenous Studies. Retrieved November 5, 2007, from www.cwis.org/fwdp/Americas/anti-ind.txt.

Guerrero, M. (1992). American Indian water rights: The blood of life in native North America. In A. Jaimes (ed.), *The state of Native America* (pp. 189–216). Boston: South End Press.

Guyette, S. (1983). *Community-based research: A handbook for Native Americans*. Los Angeles: American Indian Studies Center.

Hagan, F. (1993). *Research methods in criminal justice and criminology*. New York: MacMillan.

Herek, G., Cogan, J., and Gillis, R. (2002). Victim experiences in hate crimes based on sexual orientation. *Journal of Social Issues, 58*(2), 319–339.

Hesse, B., Rai, D., Bennett, C., and McGilchrist, P. (1992). *Beneath the surface: Racial harassment*. Aldershot, United Kingdom: Avebury Press.

hooks, b. (1990). *Yearning: Race, Gender and Cultural Politics*. Boston: South End Press.

hooks, b. (1995). *Killing rage: Ending racism*. New York: Henry Holt and Company.

Housing Assistance Council (2002). *Taking stock of rural people, poverty, and housing for the 21st Century*. Washington, D.C.: HAC.

Hunt, A. (1990). Rights and social movements: Counter-Hegemonic strategies. *Journal of Law and Society*, 17(3), 309–328.

Hurtado, A. (1997). When strangers met: Sex and gender on three frontiers. In E. Jameson and S. Armitage (eds.), *Writing the range: Race, class, and culture in the women's west* (pp. 97–142). Norman, Okla.: University of Oklahoma Press.

Iganski, P. (2003). Hate crimes hurt more. In B. Perry (ed.), *Hate and bias crime: A reader* (pp. 131–138). New York: Routledge.

Indian Nations at Risk Task Force (1991). *Indian Nations at risk: An educational strategy for action*. Washington, D.C.: United States Department of Education.

Institute for Natural Progress. (1992). In usual and accustomed places: Contemporary American Indian fishing rights struggles. In A. Jaimes (ed.), *The state of Native America* (pp. 217–240). Boston: South End Press.

Jaimes, A. (1992a). Introduction: Sand Creek: The morning after. In A. Jaimes (ed.), *The state of Native America* (pp. 1–12). Boston: South End Press.

Jaimes, A. (1992b). Federal Indian Identification Policy: A usurpation of indigenous sovereignty in North America. In A. Jaimes (ed.), *The state of Native America: Genocide, colonization, and resistance* (pp. 123–138). Boston: South End Press.

Jaimes, A. (1995). Native American identity and survival: Indigenism and environmental ethics. In Michael Green (ed.), *Issues in Native American cultural identity* (pp. 273–296). New York: P. Lang.

Jaimes, A., and Halsey, T. (1992). American Indian women: At the center of indigenous resistance in North America. In A. Jaimes (ed.), *The state of Native America: Genocide, colonization, and resistance* (pp. 311–344). Boston: South End Press.

Jefferson, T. (1994). Discrimination, disadvantage and police work. In D. Baker (ed.), *Reading racism and the criminal justice system* (pp. 243–258). Toronto, Ontario: Canadian Scholars' Press.

Jimson, T. (1992). *Reflections on race and manifest destiny*. Center for World Indigenous Studies. Retrieved November 5, 2007, from www.cwis.org/fwdp/Americas/manifest.txt.

Johnson, B., and Maestas, R. (1979). *Wasichu: The continuing indian wars*. New York: Monthly Review Press.

Johnson, T., Champagne, D., and Nagel, J. (1997). American Indian activism and transformation: Lessons from Alcatraz. In T. Johnson, D. Champagne, and J. Nagel (eds.), *American Indian activism* (pp. 9–44). Urbana, Ill.: University of Illinois Press.

Kelly, R., Maghan, J., and Tennant, W. (1993). Hate crimes: Victimizing the stigmatized. In Kelly, R. (ed.), *Bias crime: American law enforcement and legal responses* (pp. 23–47). Chicago: Office of International Criminal Justice.

Kleg, M. (1993). *Hate prejudice and racism*. Albany, N.Y.: SUNY Press.

Korsmo, F. (1999). Claiming memory in British Columbia: Aboriginal rights and the state. In T. Johnson (ed.), *Contemporary Native American political issues* (pp. 119–134). Walnut Creek, Calif: Altamira.

Levin, J., and McDevitt, J. (1993). *Hate crimes: The rising tide of bigotry and bloodshed*. New York: Plenum.

Mann, C. (1993). *Unequal justice*. Bloomington, Ind.: Indiana University Press.

Martin, S. (1994). 'Outside Within' the station house: The impact of race and gender on black women police. *Social Problems, 41*(3), 383–400.

Massey, D., and Denton, N. (1993). *American apartheid: Segregation and the making of the underclass*. Cambridge, Mass.: Harvard University Press.

McClain, P., and Stewart, J. (1995). *Can we all get along? Racial and ethnic minorities in American politics*. Boulder, Colo.: Westview.

McDevitt, J., Balboni, J., Bennett, S., Weiss, J., Orschowsky, S., and Walbot, L. (2000). *Improving the quality and accuracy of bias crime statistics nationally*. Washington, D.C.: Bureau of Justice Statistics.

McDevitt, J., Balboni, J., Garcia, L., and Gu, J. (2001). Consequences for victims: A comparison of bias- and non-bias motivated assaults. *American Behavioral Scientist, 45*(4), 697–713.

McIntosh, B. J. (1987). *Special needs of American Indian college students*. Mesa, Ariz.: Mesa Community College Office of Research and Development.

McLaren, L. M. (2003). Anti-Immigrant prejudice in Europe: Contact, threat perception, and preferences for the exclusion of migrants. *Social Forces, 81*(3), 909–936.

Messerschmidt, J. (1983). *The Trial of Leonard Peltier*. Boston: South End Press.

Mihesuah, D. (1996). *American Indians: Stereotypes and realities*. Atlanta, Ga.: Clarity Press.

Minority Student Enrollments in Higher Education. (1993). Garrett Park, Md.: Garrett Park Press.

Minow, M. (1990). *Making all the difference: Inclusion, exclusion and American law*. Ithaca, N.Y.: Cornell University Press.

Nagel, J. (2003). *Race, ethnicity, and sexuality: Intimate intersections, forbidden frontiers*. New York: Oxford University Press.

National Fair Housing Alliance (2005). *Fair housing trends report*. Washington, D.C.: National Fair Housing Alliance.

Nenadic, N. (1996). Femicide: A framework for understanding genocide. In D. Bell and R. Klein (eds.), *Racially Speaking: Feminism Reclaimed* (pp. 456–464). North Melbourne, Australia: Spinfex.

Neu, D., and Therrien, R. (2003). *Accounting for genocide: Canada's bureaucratic assault on aboriginal people*. Black Point, Nova Scotia: Fernwood Publishing.

Nielsen, M. (1996). Contextualization for Native American crime and justice. In M. Nielsen and R. Silverman (eds.), *Native Americans, crime and justice* (pp. 10–19). Boulder, Colo.: Westview.

Nielsen, M. (2000a). Native Americans and the criminal justice system. In Criminal Justice Collective (eds.), *Investigating difference: Human and cultural relations in criminal justice* (pp. 47–58). Needham Heights, Mass.: Allyn and Bacon.

Nielsen, M. (2000b). Non-indigenous scholars doing research in indigenous justice organizations: Applied issues and strategies. Paper prepared for the Western Social Sciences Association Annual Meeting San Diego, Calif., April 26–29, 2000.

Nielsen, M., and Silverman, R. (1996). (eds.), *Native Americans, crime and justice*. Boulder, Colo.: Westview.

Noriega, J. (1992). American Indian education in the United States: Indoctrination for subordination to colonialism. In A. Jaimes (ed.), *The state of Native America: Genocide, colonization, and resistance* (pp. 371–402). Boston: South End Press.

Office for Victims of Crime. (1998). *New directions from the field: Victims rights and services for the 21st Century*. Department of Justice, Washington, D.C., Office of Justice Programs.

Ogawa, B. (1999). *Color of justice: Culturally sensitive treatment of minority crime victims*. Boston: Allyn and Bacon.

Ortiz, R. (1981). Foreword. In J. Forbes (ed.) *Native Americans and Nixon: Presidential politics and minority self-determination*. Los Angeles, Calif.: American Indian Studies Center.

Osborne, S. (1995). The voice of the law: John Marshall and Indian land rights. In M. Green (ed.), *Issues in Native American cultural identity* (pp. 57–74). New York: P. Lang.

Padilla, L. (2001). "But you're not a dirty Mexican": Internalized oppression, Latinos and law. *Texas Hispanic Journal of Law and Policy*, 7 59–113.

Pavel, M. (1999). American Indians and Alaska Natives in higher education: Promoting access and achievement. In K. Swisher and J. Tippeconnic III (eds.), *Next steps: Research and practice to enhance indian education* (pp. 239–258). Charleston, W. Va.: ERIC.

Peak, K. (1997). African Americans in policing. In R. Dunham and G. Alpert (eds.), *Critical issues in policing* (pp. 356–362). Prospect Heights, Ill.: Waveland.

Perley, D. (1993). Aboriginal education in Canada as internal colonialism. *Canadian Journal of Native Education*, 20(1), 118–128.

Perlmutter, P. (1999). *Legacy of hate*. Armank, N.Y.: M.E. Sharpe.

Perry, B. (2001). *In the name of hate: Understanding hate crime*. New York: Routledge.

Perry, B. (2002). Native American victims of campus ethnoviolence. *Journal of American Indian Education*, 41(1), 35–55.

Perry, B. (2006). 'Nobody trusts them!' Under- and over-policing Native American communities. *Critical Criminology*, 14(4), 411–444.

Pertusati, L. (1997). *In defense of Mohawk Land: Ethnopolitical conflict in native North America*. Albany, N.Y.: State University of New York Press.

Poupart, L. (2002). Crime and justice in American Indian communities. *Social Justice*, 29(1/2), 144–159.

Poupart, L. (2003). The familiar face of genocide: Internalized oppression among American Indians. *Hypatia*, 18(2), 86–100.

Quesenberry, S. (1999). Recent United Nations initiatives concerning the rights of indigenous peoples. In T. Johnson (ed.), *Contemporary Native American political issues* (pp. 103–118). Walnut Creek, Calif.: Altamira.

Razack, S. (2005). Introduction: When race becomes place. In S. Razack (ed.), *Race, space, and the law: Unmapping a white settler society* (pp. 1–20). Toronto, Ontario: Between the Lines.

Reyhner, J. (1993). New directions in United States Native education. *Canadian Journal of Native Education*, 20(1), 63–75.

Riding In, J. (1998). Images of American Indians: American Indians in popular culture: A Pawnee's experiences and views, in C. R. Mann and M. Zatz (eds.), *Images of color, images of crime* (pp. 15–29). Los Angeles: Roxbury.

Riding In, J. (2002). Images of American Indians: American Indians in popular culture: A Pawnee's experiences and views. In C. R. Mann and M. Zatz (eds.), *Images of color, images of crime*, (2nd ed. pp. 14–27). Los Angeles: Roxbury.

Rittner, C. (2002). Using rape as a weapon of genocide. In C. Rittner, J. Roth, and J. Smith (eds.), *Will genocide ever end?* (pp. 91–98). St. Paul, Minn.: Paragon House.

Robbins, R. (1992). Self-Determination and subordination: The past, present and future of American Indian governance. In A. Jaimes (ed.), *The state of Native America: Genocide, colonization, and resistance* (pp. 87–122). Boston: South End Press.

Robyn, L., and T. Alcoze (2006). "The link between environmental policy and the colonization process and its effects on American Indian involvement in crime, law, and society." In J. I. Ross and L. Gould (eds.), *Native Americans and the criminal justice system* (pp. 67–84). Boulder, Colo.: Paradigm Publishers.

Roscigno, V. (1994). Social movement struggle and race, gender, class inequality. *Race, Sex and Class*, 2(1), 109–126.

Ross, L. (1998). *Inventing the savage: The social construction of Native American criminality*. Austin, Tex.: University of Texas Press.

Ross, J., and Gould, L. (eds.) (2006). *Native Americans and the criminal justice system*. Boulder, Colo.: Paradigm Publishers.

Russell, K. (1998). *The color of crime*. New York: New York University Press.

Rÿser, R. (1992). *Anti-Indian movement on the tribal frontier*. Kenmore, Wash.: Center for World Indigenous Studies.

Rÿser, R. (1993). *The anti-Indian movement in the Wise Use movement: Threatening the cultural and biological diversity of Indian country.* Center for World Indigenous Studies. Retrieved November 5, 2007, from www.cwis.org/fwdp/Americas/wiseuse.txt.

Rÿser, R. (1999). *Competing sovereignties in North America and the right-wing and anti-Indian movement.* Center for World Indigenous Studies. Retrieved April 2, 2008, from http://race.eserver.org/competing-sovereignties.html.

Saldaña-Portillo, M. (2001–2002). "'On the road' with Che and Jack: Melancholia and the legacy of colonial racial geographies in the Americas." *New Formations,* 47, 87–108.

Scheper-Hughes, N. (1996). Small wars and invisible genocides. *Social Science and Medicine,* 43(5), 889–900.

Sheehan, B. (1980). *Savagism and civility: Indians and Englishmen in colonial Virginia.* Cambridge, N.Y.: Cambridge University Press.

Sheffield, C. (1995). "Hate violence." In P. Rothenberg (ed.), *Race, class and gender in the United States* (3rd ed. pp. 432–441). New York: St. Martin's.

Silverman, R. (1996). Patterns of Native American crime. In M. Nielsen and R. Silverman (eds.), *Native Americans, crime and justice* (pp. 58–74). Boulder, Colo.: Westview.

Smith, A. (2003). Soul wound: The legacy of Native American schools. *Amnesty Magazine,* 14–16. Retrieved November 5, 2007, from http://www.libarts.ucok.edu/history/faculty/roberson/course/1493/readings/Native%20American%20Schools.htm.

Smith, A. (2005). *Conquest: Sexual violence and American Indian genocide.* Boston: South Side Press.

Smith, K. (2003). *Predatory lending in Native American communities.* Fredericksburg, Va.: First Nations Development Institute.

Smith, S. (1989). *The politics of 'race' and residence: Citizenship, segregation, and white supremacy in Britain.* Cambridge, United Kingdom: Polity Press.

Snyder-Joy, Z. (1996). Self-Determination and American Indian justice: Tribal versus federal jurisdiction on Indian lands. In M. Nielsen and R. Silverman (eds.), *Native Americans, crime and justice* (pp. 38–45). Boulder Colo.: Westview.

Stannard, D. (1992) *American holocaust.* New York: Oxford University Press.

Stiffarm, L., and P. Lane (1992). The demography of Native North America. In A. Jaimes (ed.), *The state of Native America* (pp. 23–54). Boston: South End Press.

Subcommittee on Civil and Constitutional Rights (1988). *Anti-Indian violence.* Washington, D.C.: U.S. Government Printing Office.

Subcommittee on Native American Affairs. (1994). *Law enforcement issues in the Bureau of Indian Affairs.* Washington, D.C.: U.S. Government Printing Office.

Takaki, R. (1993). *A different mirror*. Boston: Little, Brown and Co.

Takaki, R. (1994). The metaphysics of civilization: Indians and the age of Jackson. In R. Takaki (ed.), *From different shores: Perspectives on race and ethnicity in America* (pp. 52–66). New York: Oxford University Press.

Taylor, J., and Kalt, J. (2005). *American Indians on reservations: A databook of socio-economic change between the 1990 and 2000 census*. Cambridge, Mass.: Malcolm Wiener Center for Social Policy, Harvard University.

Tinker, G. (1993). *Missionary conquest: The gospel and Native American cultural genocide*. Minneapolis, Minn.: Fortress Press.

Trask, H. (2004). The color of violence. *Social Justice*, 31(4), 8–16.

United States Census Bureau (2005). *Income, poverty, and health insurance coverage in the United States: 2004*. Washington, D.C.: United States Census Bureau.

United States Census Bureau (2006). *We the people: American Indians and Alaska Natives in the United States*. Washington, D.C.: United States Census Bureau.

United States Commission on Civil Rights. (1990). *Intimidation and violence: Racial and religious bigotry in America*. Washington, D.C.: Commission on Civil Rights.

United States Commission on Civil Rights. (1992a). *Civil rights issues facing Asian Americans*. Washington, D.C.: Commission on Civil Rights.

United States Commission on Civil Rights. (1992b). *Racial and ethnic tensions in American communities: Poverty, inequality and discrimination*. Washington, D.C.: Commission on Civil Rights.

United States Commission on Civil Rights (n.d.). *Recent actions against citizens and residents of Asian descent*. Washington, D.C.: Commission on Civil Rights.

United States Department of Education and United States Department of Justice (nd), *Preventing Youth Hate Crime*. Washington, D.C.: U.S. Department of Education and U.S. Department of Justice.

Valaskakis, G. (2005). *Indian country: Essays on contemporary native culture*. Waterloo, Ontario: Wilfred Laurier University Press.

van Dijk, T. (1995). Elite discourse and the reproduction of racism. In R. Whillock and D. Slayden (eds.), *Hate speech* (pp. 1–27). Thousand Oaks, Calif.: Sage.

Varma-Joshi, M., Baker, C., and Tanaka, C. (2004). Names will never hurt me? *Harvard Educational Review*, 74(2), 175–209.

Vaughan, A. (1995). *Roots of American racism*. New York: Oxford University Press.

Wachtel, P. (1999). *Race in the mind of America*. New York: Routledge.

Washburn, W. (1995). *Red man's land/white man's law*. Norman, Okla.: University of Oklahoma Press.

Weis, L., Proweller, A., and Centri, C. (1997). Re-examining "A Moment in History": Loss of privilege inside white working class masculinity in the 1990s. In M. Fine, L. Weis, L. Powell, and L. Mun Wong (eds.), *Off white: Readings on race, power and society* (pp. 210–226). New York: Routledge.

Weisheit, R., and F. Morn (2004). *Pursuing justice*. Belmont, Calif.: Wadsworth/Thomson.

Weiss, J., Ehrlich, H., and Larcom, E. (1991–1992). Ethnoviolence at work (Institute Report #6). *Journal of Intergroup Relations, 18*(4), 21–33.

Welliver, D. (2004). Afterword: Finding and fighting hate where it lives: Reflections of a Pennsylvania practitioner. In C. Flint (ed.), *Spaces of hate: Geographies of discrimination and intolerance in the U.S.A.* (pp. 245–254). New York: Routledge.

Whaley, R., and Bressette, W. (1994). *Walleye warriors: An effective alliance against racism and for the earth.* Philadelphia, Pa.: New Society Publishers.

Whillock, R. (1995). Introduction. In R. Whillock and D. Slayden (eds.), *Hate speech* (p. xiii). Thousand Oaks, Calif.: Sage.

Whillock, R. (1995). The use of hate as a stratagem for achieving political and social goals. In R. Whillock and D. Slayden (eds.), *Hate speech* (pp. 28–54). Thousand Oaks, Calif.: Sage.

Winant, H. (1997). Where culture meets structure. In D. Kendall (ed.), *Race, class and gender in a diverse society* (pp. 27–38). Boston: Allyn and Bacon.

Wisconsin Advisory Committee to the United States Commission on Civil Rights. (1989). *Discrimination against Chippewa Indians in Northern Wisconsin.* State Advisory Committee Report. Washington D.C.: U.S. Commission on Civil Rights.

Wolfe, L., and Copeland, L. (1994). Violence against women as bias motivated crime: Defining the issues in the United States. In M. Davies (ed.), *Women and violence* (pp. 200–213). London: Zed Books.

Wright, B. (1991). *American Indian and Alaska Native higher education: Toward a new century of academic achievement and cultural integrity.* Washington, D.C.: U.S. Department of Education.

Wright, B., and Tierney, W. (1991). American Indians in higher education: A history of cultural conflict. *Change, 23*(2), 11–18.

Young, I. (1990). *Justice and the politics of difference.* Princeton, N.J.: Princeton University Press.

Young, I. (1995). Five faces of oppression. In D. Harris (ed.), *Multiculturalism from the margins* (pp. 65–86). Westport, Conn.: Bergin and Garvey.

Zatz, M., Chiago Lujan, C., and Snyder-Joy, Z. (1991). American Indians and criminal justice: Some conceptual and methodological considerations. In M. Lynch and B. Patterson (eds.), *Race and criminal justice.* Albany, N.Y.: Harrow and Heston.

Index

About the Author

Barbara Perry is a professor on the faculty of Criminology, Justice and Policy Studies at the University of Ontario Institute of Technology in Oshawa, Ontario. She has written extensively in the area of inequality and justice, with a particular emphasis on hate crime, including two books on the topic: *In the Name of Hate: Understanding Hate Crime* and *Hate and Bias Crime: A Reader*. She has just completed a book manuscript dealing with under- and overpolicing in Native American communities. Dr. Perry continues to work in the area of hate crime, and has begun to make contributions to the limited scholarship on hate crime in Canada, where she is particularly interested in anti-Muslim violence, as well as hate crime against aboriginal peoples.